# CHRISTIANITY

# CHRISTIANITY
## WHAT YOU NEED TO KNOW

RUSSELL DUMKE

Paulist Press
New York • Mahwah, NJ

Cover image by Rainer_Maiores / Pixabay.com
Cover design by Joe Gallagher
Book design by Lynn Else



Library of Congress Cataloging-in-Publication Data
Names: Dumke, Russell, author.
Title: Christianity: what you need to know / Russell Dumke.
Description: New York; Mahwah, NJ: Paulist Press, [2024] | Summary: "This book is a guide for under churched Christians to lead them to greater maturity and knowledge in their faith"—Provided by publisher.
Identifiers: LCCN 2023054196 (print) | LCCN 2023054197 (ebook) | ISBN 9780809157129 (paperback) | ISBN 9780809188673 (ebook)
Subjects: LCSH: Christianity. | Bible. | Spirituality,
Classification: LCC BR121.3 .D85 2024 (print) | LCC BR121.3 (ebook) | DDC 230—dc23/eng/20240226
LC record available at https://lccn.loc.gov/2023054196
LC ebook record available at https://lccn.loc.gov/2023054197

ISBN 978-0-8091-5712-9 (paperback)
ISBN 978-0-8091-8867-3 (ebook)

Published by Paulist Press
997 Macarthur Boulevard
Mahwah, New Jersey 07430
www.paulistpress.com

Printed and bound in the
United States of America

# CONTENTS

# ACKNOWLEDGMENTS

I wish to thank my editor, Paul McMahon, for his kind and generous help in shepherding this book into print. I also wish to thank Trace Murphy, Editor-at-Large at Paulist Press, for his magnanimous assistance with the manuscript. Ryan Masteller offered many helpful suggestions that improved the final product. To them and to everyone else at Paulist who had a hand in this project, I am grateful for helping me to realize my dream of writing a book.

# 1

# WHY THIS BOOK IS IMPORTANT

You're a Christian. You go to church regularly. Your faith or your religion is an important part of your life. Maybe it's even central to it. You have your belief, and you're all set. But are you really?

Over the years that I have been teaching religion, I've found that many people come into my classroom with a surprising lack of knowledge about their faith. It's as if they're living in a very small religious bubble. Their knowledge of Christianity is severely limited.

When I've probed this, I've typically found that the reason why is that my students received most of their religious teaching from someone in their family. This is the infamous "Grandma Syndrome": I have to believe this way because that's what Grandma pounded into me over and over again. Sometimes it was mother or some other family member doing the pounding, but the result was the same. People felt they had to believe the way they do because that's what their families made them do.

The effect of this was that people had strong beliefs, but they didn't know very much about them. They often had strong resistance to their beliefs being challenged, too. Questioning your faith was something many families simply didn't allow.

After thinking about this rather shocking state of affairs, I realized that there were certain things that were fundamental for Christians to know. These are things that I think all Christians must know if they want to grow up to full maturity in their faith. I originally had a list of three of these things, with one further thing initially being optional in my mind, but I finally realized that that fourth thing was crucial as well. That left me with four broad topics that people who are already Christian need to know about to be religiously mature.

What are these four things? Here's the list.

The first item on the list that Christians need to know about is *biblical scholarship*. That alone is a world changer. Some people may have a strong reaction to it because they see it as something that threatens their faith. To me, that's not a good place to be. There are untold riches that Bible scholars have unearthed. If you dive into this scholarship and stick to it, you'll be amazed at what you'll learn. Yes, if you take the dive, it might change your faith, but it will change it for the better.

The second item on the list is *Christian history*. Now, I don't mean only the history of your own church or denomination! I mean the history of Christianity as a whole going all the way back to the beginning. How can you know who you are as a Christian if you don't know your Christian past? It's a good thing to know your Christian roots, just as it's good to know your own family's genealogy. As a Christian, you stand on the shoulders of those Christians who came before you.

Christian history is important because you'll find a rich history of working out answers to really hard questions. We'll say more about that in our chapter on church history, but for now it's enough to know that there were conflicting ways of understanding such seemingly basic things as how Jesus saves us or what Jesus was. Getting all Christians on the same page was necessary if Christianity was to become a world religion. Of course, there are still issues today, but a lot was hashed out in the early centuries of Christianity.

The third item on the list is *worship*. Show me how you worship, and I'll tell you what you believe. Worship reveals a *lot* about how a church understands Christianity. I think you'll find that worship is far more revealing than you ever realized.

There is more to worship than what you do in church on Sunday (or perhaps another day of the week). That's because worship (the technical name for worship is *liturgy*) has to do with much more than just offering God praise. As we'll see in our chapter on worship, there is something much bigger going on. What that is involves nothing less than remaking the world into a Christian one. That's a very ambitious project, as we'll see.

The fourth and last, item on the list is *spirituality*. Christian spirituality, unfortunately, is in the same place that biblical scholarship is. Just like biblical scholarship, there is a treasure trove of Christian spiritual material that I'd wager most Christians know nothing about. Again, this material is part of every Christian's inheritance. It's there in Christian history and tradition, but many people have no idea that it even exists.

What this all boils down to is that learning about the four things on this list provides a massive potential for you to grow. Our Christian forebears left us an incredible amount of wisdom about what it means to go deep into the experience of living with God. What they gave us is extraordinarily valuable. They gave us detailed stories of what the Christian walk looks like. That can certainly benefit you today!

Every item on my list will be eye-opening if you haven't been exposed to it before. Each will likely take your religious life to a new level, and that's a big reason why this book is important. In the chapters that follow, we'll look at each one of these four topics in more detail, but first we need to set the stage for that discussion. That's what the next chapter does. In it, we'll begin to mine the riches of Christianity. We'll begin to see a fullness that's been there all along.

Once we've done that, we'll have the background to be able to take a closer look at the four areas. We'll look at each one in detail and discuss just a little of what's there in each one. Obviously, there's too much to cover in a short book like this one, but we'll be able to look at enough to give you an idea of what you may be missing. Each of the four topics will get its own chapter, and that will be the meat of the book.

When we're finished with that, I'll tie it all together at the end. I'll also have some thoughts about what we've learned and what it all means. Once you have a good grasp of the four areas, you'll be able to see how they all work together. All of that will be in the final chapter. So sit back and enjoy! I hope you find the journey through these pages to be exciting and helpful.

# 2

# HOW TO THINK ABOUT CHRISTIANITY

People are often shocked when they take my classes because they aren't used to hearing someone talk about religion the way I do. That's because they've never been exposed to the way scholars talk about religion. I have to tell them that what they will get in the course will sound different from what they got in Sunday school or wherever they got their religious instruction. I have to put in a bit of work to make people realize that there is a whole different way of talking about religion that's different, yet perfectly fine. It's just a lot more complicated than what they're used to.

Scholars talk about things in ways that are appropriate for their areas of study. The problem for religion is that there are three main areas of study that talk a lot about religion, and each is complicated in its own way. The first area of study is *theology*, the second is *religious studies*, and the third is *philosophy*. What makes things especially confusing is that there is a lot of overlap between them. Regardless, it's important to know something about each one of these areas.

Theology is the area that most people have heard of. What's distinctive about theology is that it's done from *inside* a church. In other words, the theologian is a believer and must accept the core beliefs of the church. Any theologian who claimed that Jesus was not God would probably not last very long as a theologian!

Religious studies, on the other hand, is done from *outside* all churches (indeed, from outside all religions). The religious studies scholar thus has more freedom because there are no core beliefs that he or she must have. This person may also pay more attention to aspects of religion that the theologian or philosopher might not pay as much attention to. These aspects may include things like rituals, physical objects (like vestments or chalices) that are used by religions, or even the sociological or economic aspects of religion.

Philosophy is a bit of an odd case, because the philosophical examination of religion happens primarily in a special subfield within the discipline. That subfield is, not surprisingly, known as philosophy of religion. The philosopher of religion may have the same freedom as the religious studies scholar (although there are Christian philosophers, which muddies the water even more), but he or she will sometimes use methods to study religion that are different from those used by the theologian or the religious studies scholar. These will be the methods that are common in philosophy. So, you may see lots of logic, or see religion talked about from the perspective of certain approaches to philosophy, such as continental philosophy or analytic philosophy. Things get messy here, too, because theologians and religious studies scholars often use philosophy in their own work.

Now that we have a general idea of how scholars treat religion, let's take a closer look. The theologian's job is to take what God has revealed and try to put it into some kind of order so that it's clear and coherent. That's a good idea if you want to teach people about Christianity. It's also good because it helps answer questions people might have. The religious studies scholar, on the other hand, is looking at *all* religions and trying to find out what makes each one tick. This scholar wants to know what religion is, and wants to grasp human religiosity as a whole. This person will also be on the lookout for things that religions have in common. The philosopher of religion is also interested in religion in general but will look at it through the lens of philosophy. The philosopher of religion will focus on things like whether there is any rational evidence for what a religion claims is true, or whether it's possible to prove things like the existence of God.

As you can see, there is quite a divergence of viewpoints here, which shows us just how complicated religion is. That's an important point that we'll see a lot more of as we go through the four things on my list. We're only scratching the surface!

Because this is a book about Christianity, we'll focus on theology. Now that we have a general idea of what theology does, we can look at it in more detail. This is important because the things on my list are all areas within theology.

Above, we saw that philosophers who specialize in studying religion make up the subfield of philosophy of religion. Theology has subfields in it, too. You may be surprised at how many there are!

Let's take a brief tour of these subfields, then. There are quite a few of them. Here's a list:

biblical studies
church history
patristics/patrology
pneumatology
Christology

liturgiology
Mariology
fundamental/foundational theology
dogmatic theology/systematic theology
soteriology
Christian ethics
homiletics
ecclesiology
sacramental theology
canon law
eschatology
missiology
pastoral theology
spiritual theology

That's quite a lot! They're all important, though. So let me say a few words about what each of these subfields is and what it does. That'll give us a better idea of how theologians think about Christianity.

*Biblical studies* is self-explanatory. It's the study of the Bible. This isn't the same as the home or church Bible studies you might be used to, though. It also involves much more than simply using a concordance. We'll cover biblical scholarship in depth in our next chapter, and there we're going to find out that there is a lot more to studying the Bible than you might have realized. It's an enormously complicated area of study.

*Church history* is as straightforward as it sounds. What isn't so straightforward is its contents. The history of Christianity, in all its aspects, is very rich. Our chapter on church history will cover some of this, but again, we'll barely be scratching the surface. That's because there is a history to all of the areas of theology, not to mention the political, military, and cultural history of Christianity. Two thousand years of a world religion is a lot to cover.

*Patristics*, which is also known as *patrology*, is a word that comes from the Greek or Latin word for "father." This area of theology is actually part of church history. Its focus is the study of the so-called fathers of the church. These are persons who are widely held to be famous leaders and heroes of the early church, although some people are challenging this assumption these days. The fathers were very influential in defining the church's doctrine and defeating heresies, among other important things. We'll say more about them, as well, in our history chapter.

*Pneumatology* is the area of theology that focuses on the Holy Spirit. The name may sound funny, but it comes from the Greek word for "breath," which is usually translated as "spirit." Because this area is the study of anything having to do with the Holy Spirit, things like the gifts of the Spirit (which are especially important in Pentecostal and charismatic Christianity) will be explored here.

*Christology* is like pneumatology, except that it focuses on everything having to do with Jesus instead of focusing on everything having to do with the Holy Spirit. It turns out that Jesus is much more complicated than you might think. He was God become Man, of course, but when you put those two together it raises a whole lot of questions (and a whole lot of heresies!).

Here's just one example: Jesus is perfectly human and perfectly divine. How many wills does he have, then: a human will, a divine will (God's will), or both? If your answer is that he has one will (probably God's), then congratulations—you're a heretic! You're guilty of a heresy called *Monothelitism* (which is Greek for "one will-ism"). The correct answer is that he has two wills. It isn't a problem, though, that he has two wills because Jesus's human will, perfect as it is, is always in complete harmony with his divine will.

That's just one example of what the early Christians encountered when they tried to understand and explain Jesus. It's only the tip of the iceberg, too, because many similar questions cropped up along the way. Many of the things the early church declared to be heresies had to do with Jesus. Christology covers all of that.

*Liturgiology*, as we saw earlier, is the study of worship. If you're familiar with the Roman Catholic or Orthodox traditions, then you know that they celebrate Mass. There are several forms of Mass, and there is a separate tradition surrounding each of them. How the Masses came to be and the theology each expresses is part of what liturgiologists study. We'll see that liturgy is actually more than just your worship service, though. We'll take a closer look at that when we get to our chapter on worship.

Here's a teaser, though. There are many elements that go into worship. Does your church have stained glass windows that depict people? What kind of music does it use? Does it celebrate the Lord's Supper or not, and if so, how often? Is there a regular cycle of scripture readings that your church follows, or does the person leading the service pick a passage to preach about? What kind of building does your service take place in? Is it a converted storefront, a Gothic cathedral, or something else?

The answers to these questions do more than just differentiate one church from another in what might seem like a superficial way. That's because there is a theology behind each one of these spaces, and that theology can be very detailed. Every element of worship says something about how a church understands Christianity. When we get to our chapter on worship, we'll see just how far this goes.

*Mariology* is something that's prominent in Roman Catholic theology. If the name didn't already give it away for you, this area of theology is devoted to Mary, the mother of Jesus. Devotion to Mary is strong in the Roman Catholic and Orthodox traditions.

There are several important doctrines about Mary that some churches have. An important one in Roman Catholic Mariology is that Mary was born without sin. Another is that Mary's body and soul were taken up into heaven at the end of her life. This doctrine is known as the assumption. There are other beliefs about Mary that Mariology studies, as well.

*Fundamental* or *foundational theology* is one of those disciplines where the messy interrelationship between differing ways of studying religion is on display. The culprits here are theology and philosophy. That might sound odd, but it's a matter of why philosophy is there and what it's doing. Let me explain.

I'll take a cue from the name *foundational theology* and liken the discipline to a house's foundation. Foundational theology is aimed at rational people who are not yet believers. If you can persuade these people that belief in basic things like the existence of God is reasonable, that opens the door for you to teach them the specific beliefs that your church has. These specific beliefs, which are like the house built on the foundation of the basic beliefs, are covered in *systematic* (or *dogmatic*) *theology*. Foundational theology says we need to appeal to people's reason to establish the foundation, though. That's where philosophy comes in. So you'll see something like existentialist philosophy (this is another approach to doing philosophy, and one that was popular in theology) being used to try to persuade people that it makes sense to believe in God.

*Dogmatic theology* is easy enough to understand: it deals with the teaching, or dogma, of a church. This is where you find the meaty doctrinal stuff. But what about the Bible-based churches that don't have the doctrinal depth and richness that other churches have? Do you really need other doctrinal sources if you have the Bible? The Bible should be enough for any Christian church, shouldn't it? These are the types of questions that might have sprung up in your mind.

I have a surprising answer, but it will have to wait until we get to the end of the chapter.

*Dogmatic theology* is also known in some quarters as *systematic theology*. Again, the name gives it away. It takes what God has revealed and tries to put it into some kind of order or system. There are many choices out there, and some have been around for centuries. What these theologies do is give you a comprehensive account of Christian belief and doctrine. Take this question from Christian history, for example: Are we saved by grace or by our good works? The theologian will try to answer that question in an authoritative way, and will give a detailed explanation of why he or she thinks that answer is right. That's what theology is all about.

Let me give you another example of the kind of thing that systematic theology concerns itself with. This example is actually covered by a subfield within systematic theology: *trinitarian theology*. The belief that the one God is three different persons sounds illogical, or even crazy. Trinitarian theology tries to understand both how a triune God is not a contradiction in terms, and how the three persons of the Trinity relate to one another. Such questions also came up in the early days of Christianity. Historically, there was a *very* famous split (the schism of 1054 CE) within Christianity over the way the Holy Spirit was related to the Father and the Son. But now you see how systematic theology builds on foundational theology. If you have been rationally persuaded that God exists, you are much more likely to want to hear details like these.

*Soteriology* is a discipline that you might also find within systematic theology. It's another branch of theology that gets its name from a Greek word—in this case, the Greek word for salvation. Soteriology, then, is the study of salvation. It looks at things like whether people who have never heard the gospel can ever get to heaven.

*Christian ethics* covers just what you think it does: Christian morality. Christian Ethics is different from the ethics you see in philosophy because it's guided by Christian values. Philosophical ethics is distinctive because it varies quite a bit when it comes to deciding what and why something is moral or not. Christian moral theologians often use philosophical ethics in their work, but Christian beliefs will usually allow less choice when it comes to the what and why.

*Homiletics* is a fancy word for the study of preaching. If you're Roman Catholic, you'll make the connection with the homily right away. The homily is the sermon that comes right after the reading from the Gospel in the Roman Catholic Mass.

*Ecclesiology* (this word comes from the Greek word for assembly) is an interesting area to look at. It gives you different understandings of what the church is. Is there an invisible church that is made up of all the people who are saved, regardless of the denomination they belong to? That's one theory of what the church is. Is the church intended to operate as a servant church or as the bride of Christ? These are different viewpoints. What makes a church a church, and what characteristics must a church have? These are also ecclesiological questions. They reflect different understandings of how to be Christian, as well. The different emphases on and perspectives of the people of God are what ecclesiology is all about.

*Sacramental theology* is important for those churches that have sacraments. Not all do. Generally speaking, a sacrament is something that communicates God's grace to us. This could be anything from the birth of a child to a beautiful sunset. It could also be something like marriage or holy communion. It might be the Bible. As you might expect, there is disagreement about the things that confer grace, and about how they do so.

Different churches have different views on sacraments. Like I said, some churches have them, and some don't. Some churches have more sacraments than others, too. There is also debate about just what a sacrament is and how it works. This can be a tricky thing. The discussion might turn on the fine distinction between a sign and a symbol, for example. Sacramental theology concerns itself with these matters.

*Canon law* is something that not very many people are familiar with, even if they've heard of it. The term is most familiarly associated with the Roman Catholic Church, but there are other churches, such as the Anglicans and the Methodists, that have their own legal codes. The laws such codes contain are sometimes called canons. Such legal traditions go back to the early church. In canon law, there are canon lawyers who practice much like regular lawyers do. And yes, Christians must obey these bodies of law, just like they must obey worldly law. The canons have to do with annulling marriages, disciplining the clergy, and much more. All this isn't as far-fetched as it may sound, though. The Book of Deuteronomy in the Old Testament is basically a legal code for the people of Israel.

Canon law (or its equivalent in churches that have a different name for their legal code) works similarly to the secular laws we're all familiar with. It can also be just as involved. Some churches even have their own church courts. Churches are institutions, after all, and they need to keep order within themselves. That's what canon law is for.

*Eschatology* (pronounced "ess-kuh-*tall*-uh-jee") comes from the Greek word *eschaton*. The eschaton is the last day. Eschatology, then, is the study of things pertaining to the last day. You might be familiar with different interpretations of the Book of Revelation. Lots of popular Christian books have been written about it. Eschatology is the branch of theology that focuses on those things in a more detailed way.

What *missiology* is the study of should also be clear. The name gives it away here, too. It focuses on anything having to do with missionary work. If you want to learn how to do this type of work well, you can find guidance here. This might be especially useful if you're trying to spread the Word to a much different culture.

*Pastoral theology* is a bit of a fancy term, but it's simply the study of how to be good at ministry. This can be a complicated field because ministry has to deal with difficult problems that people have. In our day and age, the kinds of problems we have are even more varied. Fortunately, pastoral theology can draw on other fields, like psychology, for help.

Finally, our last area of theology is *spiritual theology*. What this study focuses on might seem obvious, but a lot of what's in it will probably be quite different from what you expect, as I said in our last chapter. If you've never heard of "hesychasm" or "monastic rules," you're in for a surprise. That's only a small part of it, too. This material goes far beyond the inspirational or devotional books you might be familiar with from a Christian bookstore. There are radical things here—things like Christian mysticism or the Orthodox notion of *theosis* (the "divinization of man"). A lot of what spiritual theology focuses on is the experience of people who led lives in which they had very deep and profound experiences of God. There have been a *lot* of these people, and a lot of them wrote down their experiences. Some spiritual writing also describes methods Christians can use to move more fully into the spiritual life. We'll say more about this in our chapter on spirituality.

As you can see, it's possible to think about Christianity in detailed and complicated ways. Many churches tend to do this. Still, do we really need so many fields of study to understand Christianity? If my church just centers on the Bible, that's enough, right? The Bible has all the answers!

That's where a surprise comes into play. Brace yourself. It might be a shocker! Here it is: there is no such thing as pure Christianity (or pure any other religion, for that matter). It doesn't exist—never has, and never will. You might think that a Bible-centered or nondenominational church has it, but that's just not true.

The reason why is quite simple. Every church has a theology, whether it realizes it or not. In the case of a Bible-centered or nondenominational church, its theology will be an understanding of how to interpret and use the Bible. If you think that the Bible should be interpreted literally, for example, that is a theological position to take. It has a name, too. It's known as *biblicism*.

Here's a test you can take to see the truth in what I'm saying. Let someone ask you any question they want. You are only able to answer by *literally* quoting the Bible. That's it. You must answer by reading a Bible passage and not say *anything* else. The moment you say something like "what it means is" or "what God is saying is," you flunk the test. The reason why is that the minute you stop quoting the Bible word for word, you're *interpreting* it. That means you're doing theology. Even if you miraculously pass the test, though, you're still operating with a theology about how to use the Bible. You're just a better Biblicist!

There is a more common name for biblicism that I'm sure you've heard of. That word is *fundamentalism*. In Christian circles, fundamentalism is usually associated with a strict, literal interpretation of the Bible. Fundamentalism is an excellent example of what I'm talking about when I say that every church has a theology, because the reality behind Christian fundamentalism is very different from what most people think.

Fundamentalism actually originated as a term for people who accepted the teaching found in a work called *The Fundamentals: A Testimony to the Truth*. This twelve-volume work contains ninety essays. The essays carefully lay out core Christian beliefs about the Bible, as well as other topics. The authors didn't care for the kind of biblical scholarship that our next chapter will discuss. *The Fundamentals* was also meant to counter liberalism. This sounds very modern, but the first volume was actually published in 1910! The last was published in 1915.

*The Fundamentals* was given out free to hundreds of thousands of people, and it had an enormous impact. It's still available for purchase from Amazon, or you can download it for free (go to http://ntslibrary.com/New_Online_Book_Additions.htm and look for *The Fundamentals I–V*, edited by R. A. Torrey). *The Fundamentals* was seen as a strong conservative statement of faith. What you have in it, though, is scholarly work. It's very theological. That's not what we think of when we think of fundamentalism!

So biblicism might be right or it might be wrong, but it is a theology. As I said, every church has a theology, whether is thinks it does or not—even a church that takes a literalist approach to the Bible.

Here's another example. Your church might only baptize adults. You probably know that not all churches baptize only adults. Some practice infant baptism. For that matter, your church probably baptizes with water. But the Religious Society of Friends (better known as the Quakers) believes that you don't have to use water at all. For them, conversion is an inner thing.

These are all theological issues. They are matters of interpretation. The worst part is that all churches think they are following the Bible. They've all got the correct Christianity. They might even have a theology that they think proves it. But that's the larger issue here. Interpretation is the stumbling block that has dogged Christianity for centuries.

Interpretation is undoubtedly the reason why there are so many Christian denominations. You may be surprised by how many there are, though. The *World Christian Encyclopedia* famously put the number at thirty-three *thousand*. The same source suggested the number might be higher, in the forty to fifty thousand range. There is some debate about just how to define what a denomination is, but the general idea is clear. The one body of Christ is anything but.

All of this shows that different churches think about Christianity in very different ways. That's a whole lot of theology. You can also begin to see just how much thinking has been done about Christianity. This thinking hasn't just been unavoidable. It's been quite natural and intentional. Our chapter on church history will really drive home this point. First, we have to take a closer look at the Bible, though. That's what the next chapter is about.

# 3

# THE BIBLE

I'm always amused when I ask my students where the original Bible is located. After all, there has to be an original that's used for all the different versions and translations that are out there, right? The Vatican seems to be a fan favorite answer for many in my classes. Unfortunately, the real situation is much more complicated. The short answer is similar to what we saw in the last chapter about pure Christianity. In a word (pardon the pun), there is no original Bible. It doesn't exist.

Think about this for a moment. If there is no original Bible, then what do people use to make all the translations we use? They have to come from somewhere! And indeed, they do. So let's listen to the story of the Bible. Settle in, because it's not a short one.

It's true that we don't have a complete, original Bible to use for our translations. What we do have is many manuscripts of the different books of the Bible. Some of these manuscripts are incomplete, so all we have are fragments. Worse still, sometimes manuscripts of the same book are not the same. Some have extra verses. Some have errors made by the copier (remember, back then manuscripts were all handwritten). All sorts of other issues can crop up. These are obviously big problems. How do we reconcile the differences?

The answer is that scholars try to reconstruct the original Bible books as best they can. They make their best scholarly guess about the content of each original. A reconstructed book is called a *critical text. Critical* means that scholars have used scholarly methods to make the reconstructed book. To do so, they have to know things about the original languages, for example, or the history of the place the manuscript came from. The take-home point is that there is a critical text for every book of the Bible, and these critical texts are used for the translations we have.

Let's take a closer look. There are many, many manuscripts and manuscript fragments that can be used in this process, and some of them are quite small. The oldest New Testament manuscript, for example, is generally thought to be a small fragment called P52, which contains a few verses of the Gospel of John. Some were written hundreds of years before or after others. New manuscripts also turn up from time to time. The Dead Sea Scrolls, for example, found as recently as 1947, contain a large number of Old Testament manuscripts.

When I was doing my master's degree in theology, my Greek-language critical New Testament came with a foldout card with tiny print listing every manuscript that was used to make it. There were quite a lot of them. Wikipedia has a table of New Testament manuscripts that does much the same thing. You can view it here: https://en.wikipedia.org/wiki/List_of_New_Testament_papyri. The story is the same for the Old Testament. Wikipedia also has a table of Old Testament manuscripts. You can see that here: https://en.wikipedia.org/wiki/List_of_Hebrew_Bible_manuscripts. As you can see, the job of putting together a critical text is very difficult. It might seem like a miracle that it's possible to have a reconstructed Bible at all!

Sometimes the problem of reconstructing the Bible can be really serious. The Gospel of Mark provides an excellent example.

Take out your Bible and look at the ending of Mark. Does it end with Mark 16:8 or Mark 16:20? There is a longer ending of Mark that some manuscripts have, but others don't. Even worse, some manuscripts add several lines of material after verse 14. Should all of this be in the Bible or not?

Our problems don't end once we have our reconstructed Bible, though. That's because a new problem comes into play. That problem is *translation.*

It's easy to take our Bibles for granted. The old joke is that if English was good enough for Jesus, then it's good enough for me. Of course, Jesus didn't speak English, and none of the biblical manuscripts were written in it, either. The manuscripts were written in several different languages. But here's the rub: these languages are very different from most of the languages the world speaks today. Hebrew is very different from Chinese, and Greek is very different from Spanish.

Many of my students have been bilingual, and they've told me that there are things that don't translate well from Spanish to English. The same is true for the biblical languages. That's because their grammars are very different. So are things like poetic forms. The Bible I use (the *New Revised Standard Version with Apocrypha*, Oxford University Press, 1989), for example, has indented lines in it in some places to recapture some of the poetic structure of the original languages. Your Bible may well not have such indentations. Sometimes when I read Bible passages out loud to my students, I pause where there is an indent to try to convey the poetic flow of the verses. It's not easy to get, but I sometimes experience a subtle change in the meaning of a passage when I do that.

My Bible also has footnotes. That might sound shocking, but actually it's not. The footnotes include explanations for things like words that scholars don't have a clear meaning for, or translations of a different word that show up in some manuscripts. That takes us back to the problem of reconstructing the Bible again.

Most of this is hidden from view in the Bibles we commonly use, but the issues are still there. It isn't always easy to capture the meaning of something in one language when you're translating it into another. The greater the difference between languages, the greater the problem will be. Let's look at Chinese again, for example. The written Chinese language contains pictographs. That means some "letters" in Chinese are like little pictures. That's completely different from Koine (pronounced "coy-nay") Greek, which is the form of ancient Greek that much of the New Testament was written in. Koine Greek has a complex grammar. How do you translate from Koine Greek to Chinese? Won't something be lost?

Quite likely, it will. But it's even worse than that, because manuscripts of biblical books might *themselves* be written in different languages. Some manuscripts were written in a language called Syriac, for example. So now we need to translate *between* different *original* languages like Syriac and Koine Greek just to get our critical text, before we can even begin to think about translating into something like Chinese.

There is a disturbing point in all this that you might have picked up on. That point is that Christians believe that the Bible is the inspired Word of God. But now we see that just getting Bible words in any language is a vexing problem, and that translating from our best-guess reconstructions of Bible books may well cause even more meaning to drop out because of translation issues. What happens to God's Word, his revelation, then? Are these issues making us miss something that God meant us to know?

That's a thorny issue, to say the least. Even if we could read the languages the manuscripts were written in, it wouldn't completely go away. We've possibly made the problem *worse*, though—and quite deliberately! That's because our translations of the Bible don't always try to stick as close to the original languages as possible. Some translations take specific theological (there's that word again!) points of view because the translators think that will be helpful somehow. In other words, they sometimes think it's closer to what God *means.*

*The Way* was one popular version of the Bible. It was deliberately written in simple English. It didn't worry too much about sticking close to the original languages. The idea was that this translation made the Bible more accessible and easier to read and understand, and it was especially thought to be good for young people. That's a certain point of view to take. If you want to spread the Word far and wide, a translation like that could be a big help. The English of the King James Bible might not be as easy to understand.

On the other hand, inclusive Bibles have a clear theological point of view. There are several such translations now, and all of them try to use gender-neutral language. The translators of these Bibles think that doing this communicates God's message of all persons being equal in Christ. For these translators, that's part of God's revelation. You won't find that in Koine Greek, though, because words in that language are gendered.

Even the beloved King James Bible has been redone. You can now get the New King James Version of the Bible. Apparently, some people thought even the King James Version needed an update to better fit the times.

So translating the Bible is actually a lot more complicated than you might have realized. We'd have enough headaches if that was all we had to worry about. Unfortunately, we're only getting started. There are more wrinkles to the Bible story.

Here's the next one. The various books of the Bible were written over a period of hundreds of years. Each was written for people who were alive at the time it was written. However, different books were written in different cultures. The audiences in those cultures would have understood the cultural references in them.

The Bible (I'll simplify here to include the whole Bible, even though what I'm going to say is true for every book in it) moved out of those times, though. As it moved through history, it moved into different cultures. The Middle East of the first couple of centuries after Jesus's time was much different from medieval Europe, for example. As a result, those original cultural understandings were lost. People interpreted the Bible through the lens of the culture they lived in, instead of through the lens of the original culture. That means that some things in the Bible took on a meaning that was different from what the original author intended.

By the time the Bible reached our time, quite a lot of this had occurred. Now, our understanding of the Bible has potentially strayed far from the original meaning. Once again, we run the danger of misunderstanding God's Word and missing what God actually reveals in the Bible. The antidote for this has been to come up with a way to interpret the Bible that will get us back to the original meaning. That way is known as the historical-critical method of biblical interpretation.

The historical-critical method tries to get back to the original meaning of the books of the Bible. Some Christians might not think this is necessary. They might even find it threatening. Doesn't the Bible say that the Holy Spirit will keep us in the truth? This is a good example of why biblical scholarship can make a huge difference in your faith life. Let me give you another example.

First Corinthians 6:13–20 is a passage that famously says that no one should have sex with a prostitute. The meaning looks clear to us. However, "prostitute" means something quite different in its original historical context!

It's quite possible that what the word in this passage originally referred to was a sacred prostitute or temple prostitute. These were women who had sex as a means of devotion or worship to a particular goddess. This sex was religious. Sometimes it was linked to fertility cults. In such a case, the idea was that having sex would encourage the appropriate deity to grant fertility to the people's herds and crops. Obviously, these were things they needed to survive. Religiosity of this kind was common in the ancient Middle East and areas around it, and it has a long history, going back even to Old Testament times.

This passage, therefore, may not be so much about sexual morality as it is about people keeping one foot in Christianity and the other in a different religion. Paul obviously had a problem with this and wanted to keep the church in Corinth focused on being Christian. First Corinthians 6:13–20 can be seen as more about identity, then, than it is about sex.

As you can see, there's a big difference between the way this passage is often understood today and what it originally meant to the church at Corinth to whom this letter was originally sent. You can see that the teaching around this passage would change dramatically if the person doing it was familiar with what biblical scholarship has found. Repeat this kind of example for other Bible books and scripture verses and you will have a very different understanding of the Bible at the end of the day. This understanding might differ quite a bit from what you've been taught, but if you're willing to look at the scholarship, the richness you'll find could really deepen your understanding and your faith.

The historical-critical method of interpreting the Bible is quite valuable. It's not the only method that biblical scholarship has at its disposal to interpret the Bible, though. There are many more methods that are being used today. These methods typically focus on a very specific approach. Rhetorical criticism, for example, looks at how authors of various parts of the Bible use rhetorical forms (these are essentially ways of making speeches) to communicate their message.

Sometimes biblical authors took material that was already there and modified it for their own purposes. Scholars must look at that, as well. Perhaps the most famous example is the story of the flood in the book of Genesis. Flood stories had been around for quite awhile by the time Genesis was written. They originated from the ancient Sumerian culture. It's quite possible that the author of Genesis took that story and gave it a new twist that was meant for his specific audience.

There are still more ways that scholars interpret the Bible. Earlier we saw that inclusive Bibles try to more faithfully (in the eyes of the translators, at least) give us God's revelation. In a similar vein, we now have feminist analysis, queer analysis, and disability analysis, to name a few. There's also a method that looks at how material that was originally handed down orally kept its form in the Bible. All of these seek to provide a clearer understanding of just what God is trying to tell us in the scriptures.

The list doesn't stop here, but I think the point is clear. Different ways of trying to interpret the Bible, along with related studies in archaeology, history, anthropology, and sociology, have greatly expanded our knowledge of God's Word. These things have added a lot to our understanding of the Bible.

There's a side note that I want to include here because it bears on the issue of how the Bible has been understood and used. The Bible is actually a collection of many different kinds of writings. A gospel is not the same thing as an epistle, and the legal material in Deuteronomy is not the same as the apocalyptic material in Revelation. Different kinds of writings have different purposes. That should be obvious, but it's important to keep these differences straight when using the Bible. Otherwise you might use some of it in the wrong way. Just because it's all inspired doesn't necessarily mean you can mix and match verses at will. The danger is obvious: you might take things wildly out of context and wind up making the Bible mean something other than what it's supposed to mean. Biblicism is especially likely to do that.

Unfortunately, some people think it's OK to do that. They have no problem with cherry-picking different verses from different books of the Bible and presenting the result as authoritative teaching. Another name for this way of using the Bible is "proof texting." It's called that because you string together a bunch of inspired verses and use them as "proof" for something. As you can see, this way of using the Bible ignores the deeper understanding of what's going on in the Bible that we have been talking about here. It's very easy to misinterpret the Bible when you proof text.

Our Bible story isn't quite finished yet, however. There is one more thing we need to look at, and it's just as big as anything we've already talked about. This might surprise you even more!

I'll start by asking you to consider your Bible. You might want to grab it and take a look. It's the Bible, of course—God's Word. The Bible is the Bible. It's the inspired Word of God that all Christians base their faith on.

Well, not so fast! I always get a kick out of telling my students that I am the only one in the room who has a complete Bible. Everyone else doesn't. (I'm actually not quite correct about that, but I'll say why later.) And while this statement is a little misleading, it makes the point. You may be shocked to find out that there isn't just one Bible Christians use. In fact, there are *five*. I don't mean five different translations, either. I'm talking about *five different Bibles*. My Bible is "complete" because it includes all of the contents of four of these. The situation with the fifth is a special case, as I'll explain later.

What we're talking about now is the biblical *canon*. Here, the word "canon" means the list of books that are accepted as being divinely inspired scripture. In other words, we're talking about the list of books that make up the Bible. As I mentioned above, there are five of these canons. Which canon you use depends on which Christian church you're talking about. The Bible you use therefore depends upon the canon your church accepts.

The Bible I use has a list of the four canons used by churches. My Bible includes all of the books on the list. That's why I'm the one in the room with the (mostly) complete Bible.

So what are the differences between the four Bibles on my Bible's list? Most of them involve changes to the Old Testament. My Bible describes them as follows: The first Bible includes books and additions that are in the Roman Catholic, Greek, and Slavonic Bibles. The second Bible includes books in the Greek and Slavonic Bibles but not included in the Roman Catholic canon. The third Bible includes texts that are in the Slavonic Bible and the appendix to the Roman Catholic Vulgate (the Vulgate is an influential Latin version of the Bible that was translated by Saint Jerome), and the fourth Bible includes an appendix to the Greek Bible. The specific breakdown looks like this:

A. Books and additions to Esther and Daniel that are in the Roman Catholic, Greek, and Slavonic Bibles:
    - Tobit
    - Judith
    - The Additions to the Book of Esther
    - Wisdom of Solomon
    - Ecclesiasticus, or the Wisdom of Jesus Son of Sirach

Baruch
The Letter of Jeremiah (= Baruch chapter 6)
The additions to the Book of Daniel
- The Prayer of Azariah and the Song of the Three Jews
- Susanna
- Bel and the Dragon

1 Maccabees
2 Maccabees

B. Books in the Greek and Slavonic Bibles but not in the Roman Catholic canon
- 1 Esdras (= 2 Esdras in the Slavonic Bible and = 3 Esdras in the appendix to the Vulgate)
- Prayer of Manasseh (in the Vulgate appendix)
- Psalm 151
- 3 Maccabees

C. Book in the Slavonic Bible and in the appendix to the Latin Vulgate
- 2 Esdras (= 3 Esdras in the Slavonic Bible and = 4 Esdras in the Vulgate appendix)

D. Book in an appendix to the Greek Bible
- 4 Maccabees

My Bible, then, includes the complete text of all the books found in the Protestant, Roman Catholic, Greek, and Slavonic Bibles. You may have heard that Catholics have seven more books in their Bible than Protestants have, but this goes way beyond that. How could this have happened?

The answer has to do with church history, which is one of the four things I said all Christians who are serious about growing in their faith should know. Specifically, we're talking about a part of that history that has to do with canon formation. In plain language, what this means is that there was a long and complicated process through which the Bible became the Bible, and this process differed from place to place. The Bible didn't fall down from heaven complete and finished!

To begin with, you need to know that there were *many* Christian writings in the early days of the church. We'll say more about that in our next chapter. There were many different kinds of writings, as well. As a matter of fact, there were several gospels that didn't make it into the New Testament. You may have heard of the Gospel of Thomas, or maybe even the Gospel of Judas. But have you ever heard of the Gospel of Peter or the Gospel of Philip? Bart D. Ehrman's book *Lost Christianities: The Battles for Scripture and the Faiths We Never Knew* (Oxford, 2003) lists sixteen different gospels that didn't become scripture. Adding the Gospel of Judas to the list, that makes *seventeen* gospels that never made it into the New Testament. Only four did.

Now, there's an important point to keep in mind here: In the early church, the scriptures were the Jewish scriptures—in other words, the Old Testament. Christians wrote a lot of their own works, but for quite a while most Christians weren't terribly bothered by the variety of different writings that were in use. They just used what they liked. There wasn't any idea that there was, or ought to be, a New Testament. Over time, various works stood out and were held in higher regard. People thought they were particularly useful. Eventually, they were considered to be inspired.

This brings us back to the fathers of the church, whom I mentioned in chapter 2. Some of them wrote lists of books they thought were good for Christians to use. These lists were influential in getting us to the Bibles we use today. These lists varied, though, and none of them completely reflects the New Testament we have now.

These lists solidified over time. Eventually, church councils took up the matter and made official pronouncements. This was another step in the overall process.

Church councils (we'll say more about these in our next chapter) discussed the canon over a long period of time. The first to really do so was the Council of Laodicea in the fourth century CE. ("CE" stands for "Common Era." It's the same thing as "AD," or "anno Domini." Similarly, "BCE" stands for "before the Common Era." It's the same thing as "BC," or "before Christ.") That's almost four hundred years after Jesus walked the earth. The Roman Catholic canon wasn't officially set until the Council of Trent in the sixteenth century, and this event was essentially a response to the Reformation.

Geography, language, and local custom also played a large role in how different Christian churches formed their canons. As I mentioned before, some churches simply had different ideas about different books. And that brings us to our fifth Bible: the Bible used by the Ethiopian Orthodox Tewahedo Church. This Bible is unusual because it has a narrow canon and a broad canon. The broad canon has books that are not found in any other Christian Bible. Unfortunately, the English translation of this Bible is apparently unfinished. It is because of this, along with the unusual view of canonicity of the Ethiopian Orthodox Tewahedo Bible, that my statement about having the only complete Bible in my classroom is qualified with "mostly."

Canon formation was a messy process, as you can see. Some people considered certain books to be scripture, while others didn't. Many books that were very popular with early Christians never made it into any canon. They are all but forgotten now. And then there are some people who even think that there has been new revelation from God in *recent* times.

If you think about it, God certainly could reveal more of himself now if he wanted to. It certainly isn't impossible. The Mormons (the Church of Jesus Christ of Latter-day Saints) believe this has happened. You may have heard of the *Book of Mormon*. You probably have not heard of the *Pearl of Great Price*. Historically, these are recent books, but both are scripture for Mormons.

There is also *A Course in Miracles*. The "author" of this book, Helen Schucman, claimed that Jesus dictated its contents to her. If you believe that, then it is yet another revelation from God. You might not be familiar with *A Course in Miracles*, but it's been quite popular with people who are in Alcoholics Anonymous.

So where does all of this leave us? I think it leaves us with two important questions to consider. The first should be obvious: Does my Bible contain books it shouldn't, or is it missing any books it is supposed to have? That's a disturbing proposition. The short answer is that answering it gives you a glimpse of just how diverse and complicated Christianity really is.

The second question has to do with something we have so far avoided talking about: the question of divine inspiration. We are fond of saying that God inspired the Bible, but do we really know how that works? Did God whisper in someone's ear, dictating the words he wanted us to read? The manuscript situation suggests that this is not what happened. Did God seize control of the writers and cause automatic writing to happen? Again, the manuscript situation doesn't seem to support this idea. Did human authors have no idea that they were divinely inspired when they wrote? That seems more likely. We still have the problem of different canons, though. After all, the canon problem is really one that has to do with divine inspiration. It's the problem of determining which books are divinely inspired and which are not.

You may have heard that the Holy Spirit somehow guides Christians. But there are theologies that defend the idea that only "our" church is right, and the others are wrong. Now we have a better understanding, though. It's not just issues over the "correct" interpretation of scripture we have to worry about, but it's even the issue of what's *in* the scriptures—what books are scripture and which not. Still, battles shouldn't happen over these issues, should they?

For whatever reason, Christianity isn't unified. Things are both messier and richer than you may have realized. This is why biblical scholarship (and church history) is so central to understanding Christianity, even if that's not apparent on the surface. We've seen that what's going on with the Bible is much more involved, and there have been real consequences because of that. Hopefully, you now have some new ideas about what to study when it comes to the Bible, and of what that study can do for your faith walk.

# 4

# CHRISTIAN HISTORY

If you were to ask me who the three most important people in Western cultural history are, I would say Plato, Aristotle, and Jesus Christ. I'm sure I would get no argument over the last name on my list, but the other two might sound puzzling. Why are two old Greek philosophers so important?

The answer is really going to surprise you if you're not familiar with Christian history. That's because a couple of funny things happened along the way in the history of Christianity, and our two Greeks had a lot to do with that.

The first thing that happened was a marriage that took place early in church history. Now, I'm not talking about an actual marriage between two people but a broader marriage of sorts, and one that was just as intimate. That marriage was the marriage of Christianity and Plato's philosophy.

Most people are not aware of the fact that Plato's philosophy had a *huge* influence on the emerging Christian church. There is a very good reason why this was so. In the early days of the church, people had many different ideas about Jesus and about Christianity. This wasn't a big problem until the Roman emperor Constantine decided to make Christianity the official religion of the Roman Empire. To make that work, he had to get all the Christians on the same page with respect to what they believed. Remember, there was no New Testament he could appeal to in order to do so. So the leaders of the church reached for the tools that were available to them. Those tools were found in Greek philosophy.

You may recall that when we discussed Monothelitism, we saw that this was just one example of the kinds of issues the early church had to resolve. Another big one right at the start also had to do with Jesus. This time, there was a fourth-century bishop named Arius who taught that Jesus wasn't eternal. He was the first and best of God's creations, but, as the Arian saying went, "there was when He was not." This teaching was very influential for a time, but there were bishops who opposed it. This all came to a head at the great Council of Nicaea.

Nicaea was a city in what is now Turkey, and the council held there was the first of what are known as *ecumenical councils*. At ecumenical councils, all the bishops from the entire church come together to exercise their teaching authority. These were crucial for setting the direction of Christianity. They have continued since the early days of the church, too, but there are complications: some churches accept the teaching of all the ecumenical councils, whereas others accept the teaching of only some of them. Some churches don't accept the teaching of any of them.

At any rate, the First Council of Nicaea was held in 325 CE. The council decided that Arius's teaching was heretical. It also wrote a statement of faith called the Nicene Creed, which, as you can see, is named after the council. This statement is still recited today at every Roman Catholic Mass.

The Nicene Creed contains a line about Jesus that says he is "one in substance with the Father." This line was the council's answer to Arius. This line is also an example of Greek philosophy coming into play.

The word "substance" is a translation of the Greek word *ousia* (pronounced "ooh-*see*-ah"). Ousia is a technical term from Greek philosophy. It means the essence of a thing, or whatever makes that thing what it is. Whatever it is that makes a pen a pen is the essence, or substance, of the pen. So when the Council of Nicaea declared that Jesus has the same substance as the Father, it was saying that the Father and Jesus were made of the same stuff. They shared the same essence. Whatever made the Father God was what made Jesus God. That makes them one. Of course, this also meant that Jesus is eternal.

You can see, then, that the Council of Nicaea used Greek philosophy to make an important theological point. The word *ousia* allowed the bishops to do this with the precision they needed.

That's hardly the end of Greek philosophy's influence on Christianity, though, and especially of Plato's influence. Plato is responsible for something even more startling: the Christian understanding of the soul.

We're used to the idea that we are made up of a body and a soul. When we die, our soul will go to heaven or hell. That's standard Christian teaching. However, this teaching isn't biblical. You won't find it in scripture. The reason why is that it comes from Plato.

The Bible teaches bodily resurrection. You may recall that puzzling passage in 1 Corinthians 15 that discusses the resurrection body. According to the Gospels, Jesus was also resurrected. Resurrection is in the Old Testament as well.

The body is a physical thing. However, according to the biblical view of resurrection, it's also a single thing. You are your body. Your body and your mind are one. This teaching is true for both testaments. There was no body left in the tomb after Jesus' resurrection. His soul didn't leave it behind!

If resurrection is what's in the Bible, where did the body/soul idea come from? The answer is that it came from one of Plato's dialogs—specifically, the *Phaedo.*

Plato didn't write textbooks or scholarly books as we understand them. He wrote dialogs, which—just as the word implies—are works where a cast of characters has a conversation with one another about some important topic. In the *Phaedo*, the topic is the immortality of the soul. This topic was important because the *Phaedo* portrays the discussion Socrates (another important Greek philosopher who was Plato's teacher) had on the day he was executed.

Let's backtrack a bit. The Greek word for soul is *psyche.* This is the word we get our word *psychology* from. In Greek, *psyche* means "mind or soul." This word is in both Plato's teachings and the New Testament.

We typically think of our souls as immaterial versions of ourselves, but that's not quite what the Greek word means. For Plato, the soul is not just immaterial and immortal. Among other things, it's also the rational part of us. There also are other characteristics that only our souls have, and Plato discusses these in detail in his dialog the *Phaedrus.* These characteristics make it different from the body. So you see, Plato's view is really the opposite of the resurrection view.

In the *Phaedo*, Plato describes death as the separation of the soul from the body. That certainly sounds familiar! The body will eventually be gone because it is an impermanent material thing. It will decompose. The soul, on the other hand, cannot be destroyed. That's what immortality means. One reason why is that it is simple, which means it's not made up of more basic parts that will eventually break apart and separate from one another.

The question, then, is what happens to the soul after it is separated from the body at death. Where does it go? That's where Plato's worldview enters the picture.

In simple terms, Plato's world looks like a layer cake with two halves (it actually has more parts than that, but we'll stick with the two big ones). The bottom half is the familiar material world we all inhabit right now. Plato calls this the realm of *Becoming*. It's physical, and it's always changing. Nothing in it is permanent. The top half is filled with only immaterial things. It's not physical, and the things in it are unchanging. Plato calls this the realm of *Being*. This is where we find the substances (the ousias) we talked about earlier.

Unfortunately, our souls are in the wrong place. They are immaterial and immortal things trapped in an ever-changing physical world. It's easy to see that our souls properly belong in the top half of Plato's worldview. If we live correctly, our souls will separate from our bodies at death and enter into the realm of Being. We need to live life a certain way for that to happen, though, and that requires discipline.

For Plato, that discipline means practicing how to die. This doesn't mean you should prepare for suicide! What it does mean is this: Plato lays the ills of the world at the feet of the body. Its desires for fancy clothes and sexual pleasure, for example, can cause all sorts of problems and keep the soul from focusing on the realm of Being, which is where it belongs. Disease can trouble the physical body as well. If death is the separation of the soul from the body, finally freeing it to hopefully go where it belongs, why not separate the two as much as we can *before* we die so that our souls will more easily go there at death? Embracing a discipline that separates the body from the soul, then, is a good idea.This idea has been very influential for Christianity, as we'll see in our chapter on spirituality.

This way of looking at things is *dualistic*. That means that there is a stark contrast between the material and the immaterial.

In Christian terms, this will become the contrast between matter and spirit. The material world is the fallen world that is the place of temptation and sin, whereas the spiritual world is free of those things. The two are opposites that conflict with each other.

You can see how Plato's ideas would be very attractive to Christians. Plato's worldview and Christianity's worldview are similar in many ways. If Plato's worldview sounds a lot like a distinction between heaven and earth, then you're on the right track. That's not quite the way Plato understands it, but it's close.

Plato's emphasis on living a certain kind of life will sound very familiar to Christians, too. All agree that it's better to focus on a heavenly good that is better than any earthly one. The spiritual good will never change, whereas earthly goods don't last forever. The spiritual good is what we're made for.

Plato's conception of the soul didn't just influence Christianity. It did the same thing for Judaism, thanks to a philosopher named Philo of Alexandria. Plato and Aristotle also had a massive influence on Islam, but that's another story. Still, you can now begin to see just how influential our two Greeks were.

The story doesn't end there, though. It continues with Neoplatonism (literally "new Platonism"). As the name suggests, Neoplatonism sought to develop Plato's philosophy more fully. It even attempted to unify Plato's thought with Aristotle's. Neoplatonism was very influential with several of the church fathers. Many of them used it in their writings. It was the language they spoke when they discussed matters of belief and doctrine. Neoplatonism also had a tremendous influence on Christian spirituality, as we'll see in our chapter on that.

In various forms, Platonic philosophy was arguably the hugest driver of Christian theology up until the thirteenth century. That's when an upstart rebel (some of his work was condemned by the bishop of Paris) knocked Plato off his throne. The rebel's name should be familiar to you if you're Roman Catholic. His name is Thomas Aquinas. If you're Catholic, you might know him as St. Thomas Aquinas, Doctor of the Church.

What Aquinas did was make a new marriage. This time the marriage was not between Plato and Christianity. Instead, it was between Aristotle and Christianity. Aquinas (he is often simply referred to as Thomas) forged a new synthesis between Christian belief and Aristotle's philosophy. This synthesis was so successful that it became the doctrine of the Roman Catholic Church up until the mid-twentieth century. That's roughly seven hundred years. It was only after the Second Vatican Council (Vatican II) in the early 1960s, which was another of the great ecumenical councils, that the door was opened for more contemporary theology.

Aquinas largely shaped a new view of the world. He was able to do this because Aristotle's philosophy was so complete. However, much of it had been lost to the Western world up until Aquinas's time. It survived in the Islamic world, however. Thomas was fortunate because he had Latin translations of Aristotle's formerly lost works at his disposal.

Aquinas thus gave the world a Christianized version of Aristotle's philosophy. This was very handy. It allowed the church to answer many vexing questions, one of which was about the Lord's Supper. This question asked how the bread and wine could become the body and blood of Christ while still seeming to be just bread and wine. This question was asked in a time before the Protestant churches existed, and Christians believed that Jesus was really present in the bread and wine. Celebrating the Lord's Supper (also known as holy communion) wasn't just a memorial service.

The answer put forth by Aquinas had to do with Aristotle's explanation of the causes of material things. Aristotle said that there are four causes for every material object. We only need to focus on two of them here, though. The first is called the material cause, which is simply the physical matter that makes up a thing. The second is the formal cause. The formal cause is nothing less than the substance or essence, or the ousia, that we talked about earlier. It's called the formal cause because Plato called substances or essences "Forms." Aristotle reworked Plato's philosophy but kept the general idea of the Forms when he did.

So for Aristotle, the bread is composed of physical stuff, and there is a substance or essence of bread that turns that physical stuff specifically into *bread* physical stuff. The same is true for wine. There is the physical stuff and then the *wine* essence or substance that specifically turns the physical stuff into *wine* physical stuff.

The problem of the real presence of Jesus in the bread and wine then became easy to solve. It was a special case. During Mass, the bread and wine keep their appearance (the physical stuff) as bread and wine, but the *substances* of bread and wine are swapped out for the *divine* substance. You may recall that the church already determined that Jesus was the same substance as the Father, so once the swap of substances within the bread and wine is complete, people are literally able to take in and connect with God. That's why it's called holy communion. You can spiritually connect or commune with God if God is really there in the bread and wine. It's a way to take God into your soul.

Here's another example of Aristotle's influence on Christianity. You may be familiar with the notion that Christians should have faith, hope, and charity (charity means love). These are sometimes called the theological virtues. It turns out that Aquinas discusses these prominently in his writing.

Here's the story. Part of what Aristotle wrote about was ethics. He came up with a famous approach to ethics called *virtue ethics*. As you might expect, a key part of this theory centers on certain virtues that people are supposed to embody. When Aquinas Christianized Aristotle, he Christianized Aristotle's ethics as well. What Thomas did was take Aristotle's list of virtues, which were things that the Greeks valued, and swap them out for the three Christian virtues: faith, hope, and charity. These three things, then, are virtues that Christians should strive to embody, and Aquinas was able to flesh out the Christian understanding of what it means to embody them using Aristotle's ethical framework.

Of course, Plato and Aristotle had a wider influence on the world that wasn't limited to Christianity. The way of classifying living creatures into genus and species came from Aristotle, for example, and this scheme is still used today. But now you can begin to see the bigger picture of how these two philosophers influenced Christianity. For roughly thirteen hundred years, Christian doctrine was largely done in the key of Plato, to use a musical metaphor. Then for roughly seven hundred years after that, it was done in the key of Aristotle. There are still people today who believe that Thomas Aquinas got it right, and there have been several theologians who have tried to update him for our times.

So far, our history has focused on Christianity's efforts to unify itself and its teachings. We haven't paid as much attention to the historical circumstances that led to these efforts. It's time to take a look at them. What you'll find is that early Christianity was much wilder than you probably knew. In fact, there are parallels with the wide range of Christian beliefs that you find today.

Let's start at the beginning. Christianity actually began as a movement within Judaism. It wasn't a world religion right away! It took some time before that happened.

The event that really opened the door for Christianity to spread around the world was the famous council described in Acts 15. There it was decided that people did not need to be circumcised and did not need to keep the Jewish laws in order to be Christian. Those things were obviously essential for Jews. But with those requirements removed, Christianity was able to spread to the Gentiles.

And spread it did. However, that messy word *interpretation* came into the picture. Despite the efforts of Paul and the other writers of the New Testament epistles, groups of people all over the Roman world had very different views of what Jesus and Christianity were all about.

Let me give you a few examples. These will give you an idea of the diversity that was present in early Christianity. They'll also show you some of the issues that the early church had to deal with.

We'll begin with the Ebionites. This group evidently didn't get the memo from the council described in Acts 15. The Ebionites were Jews and thought you needed to be Jewish to be Christian. They kept the Jewish laws that Acts 15 says the Gentiles didn't need to follow. Some Ebionites might not have believed in Jesus's virgin birth, either. They thought Joseph and Mary had sex and conceived Jesus that way. They apparently used their own version of the Gospel of Matthew, which denied the virgin birth. This version reflected their particular beliefs.

The Ebionites weren't the only group of early Jewish Christians. There were others as well, like the Nazarenes. All were eventually deemed to be heretical. It's interesting to note that Jewish Christianity in some sense survives today, however. There are messianic Jews in our world now. These are Jews who accept Jesus as the Messiah.

A much different group of early Christians was known as the Marcionites. This group's beliefs found wide appeal. The Marcionites really didn't like the Jewish influence in Christianity and didn't use the Old Testament. That's because, for them, there wasn't one God. There were *two*. There was the God of the Old Testament, who wasn't a very nice fellow, and the God of the New Testament, who was much better.

Marcion (the founder of the group) also had his own canon of scripture. Some of the books in it were edited quite a bit. His teaching was heavily influenced by Paul (whom the Ebionites totally rejected). Still, Marcionism was also declared to be heretical, and Marcion was excommunicated in 144 CE. It's interesting to see how the Ebionites and the Marcionites were poles apart, yet both suffered the same fate.

This is where the fathers of the church really began to exert their historical influence. People like Iranaeus, Tertullian, and Clement of Alexandria were instrumental in combating perceived heresies, shaping Christian belief, and setting the canon of scripture. That's much of what they did. There were a great many of these writers, too. Luckily, we have English translations of their writings. These are now freely available on the internet. You can read them here: https://www.ccel.org/fathers.

Yet another early Christian group (actually several different groups more or less united by a common theme, and some of them possibly not Christian) was the Gnostics. This group of people had a very different take on salvation.

To begin with, the Gnostics were arguably influenced by Greek philosophy more than any other group. They took the opposition between matter and spirit very seriously. This dualism (dualism meaning that there are just two basic kinds of stuff that make up the universe) led them to a position very much like Plato's. For the Gnostics, the material world is a terrible place that needs to be escaped from. It was created by a lesser being called the Demiurge. There is also a superior, spiritual place above this world where our souls came from that our souls need to get back to. For the Gnostics, we lost our spiritual awareness as our souls descended through more limiting levels of the world.

The problem is how to get back to that superior, spiritual place. Humanity has lost its way. Jesus knew the way back, however, and that's what he came to give us. For Christian Gnostics, it was this saving *knowledge* (the term *Gnostic* comes from the Greek word *gnosis*, which means "knowledge") that is our salvation. Dying on the cross and being resurrected had absolutely nothing to do with it. After all, the body is a material thing. It needs to be left behind.

This shocking idea is obviously out of step with mainstream Christianity, for which the death and resurrection of Jesus are central. And for the early church, this was yet another interpretation of Christianity, and one that posed a big problem.

The Gnostics wrote quite a few books of their own, including Gospels. The most famous collection of these books is the Nag Hammadi Library. These books also include material that claims to have come from Jesus. You can see how this might cause problems, but the problems are not limited to Gnostic texts. Textual issues raised by these groups bear directly on canon formation.

Christian Gnosticism was also condemned by several church fathers. Iranaeus, the bishop of Lyon, wrote an especially well-known refutation of Gnosticism. Other church fathers like Tertullian followed him. Gnosticism joined the list of expressions of Christianity that were historically acceptable for one moment and deemed heretical the next.

There is one last group I want to mention in order to illustrate just how wide open early Christianity was. This was a sect called the Carpocratians. This group, which was also named after its founder (whose name was Carpocrates), believed in reincarnation. They were also known for their wild sexual permissiveness. Apparently, they believed that one must experience as much as they can in this life in order to avoid reincarnating to finish the job. They also seem to have believed that nothing is immoral. You may think this theology is awful and thoroughly not Christian, but Carpocratian ideas, too, survive today.

The Carpocratians were not the only Christians in the ancient world who believed in reincarnation. Origen was a very influential Christian writer (his views were later determined to be not fully acceptable, but he was quite influential in his time) who saw no problem with Christianity embracing the concept. There are also people who have recently argued that reincarnation is not incompatible with Christianity. As for the idea that nothing is immoral and everything is permitted, it, too, is still around. There are churches that teach "once saved, always saved." The proper term for this teaching is *antinomianism* (which means "anti-law-ism"). For these Christians, once you have been saved, it is impossible for you to go to hell. You can do anything and never lose your salvation. In that sense, at least, morality no longer applies to you.

In fact, some early Christians believed that even those in hell would eventually be saved. No one would ever be permanently lost. This teaching is known as universal salvation or universalism. It, too, is still alive.

It's important to repeat that all these groups in the early church considered themselves to be Christians. Without any commonly accepted New Testament, how was the church supposed to sort out all of these different beliefs? Historically, the process was long and involved. The chief means for shaping the church's doctrine were the ecumenical councils, which I've mentioned before.

Remember, these are councils where all the church's bishops gathered together to settle matters of doctrine. As I mentioned before, these were crucial for ironing out the issues posed by all the different Christian beliefs that existed in early Christianity. They also illustrate the way authority was understood and exercised in Christian history pretty much up until the Reformation in the sixteenth century. A pope would call for an ecumenical council and had to accept its decisions and teachings. That's because the pope was seen as the head of the church. If he didn't put his official stamp of approval on a council's work, it wasn't official church doctrine.

The Roman Catholic Church teaches that there have been twenty-one ecumenical councils. Eastern Orthodox Christianity only accepts the first seven of these, however. This has much to do with the first great split in Christianity, which occurred between these two churches in 1054 CE. To make matters even more complicated, the Roman Catholic Church only accepts parts of what some of these councils decided as being official doctrine. That's because only those parts meet its conditions for being promulgated by an ecumenical council.

You can find a list of the twenty-one councils here: https://www.newadvent.org/library/almanac_14388a.htm. If you look closely, you'll see that many of them dealt with various heresies. Persons teaching such heresies were typically *anathematized* (that means the teaching and the person teaching it is denounced by ecclesiastical authority as *really* unacceptable and won't be tolerated *at all*). This is how the early church dealt with many questions and challenges. The councils were critical for keeping discipline and order within the church's ranks.

One of the most famous examples of all this was the Council of Trent in the sixteenth century. This council was the Western (or the Roman Catholic) Church's response to the Reformation. The Reformation was, of course, the time when several Protestant churches were formed. As the word *Reformation* suggests, its adherents (people like Martin Luther) tried to change the church because they saw abuses taking place within it. They protested against what they thought was wrong. When the Western Church refused to accept what the reformers were calling for, the groups who followed the reformers split off from it and formed their own denominations.

The reformers often had different theological points of view from the Roman Catholic Church. To continue with the example of Martin Luther, he believed that the Bible should be the sole authority for Christians. Many churches today follow that lead. To this day, however, the Roman Catholic Church insists on two sources of authority: scripture and tradition. Luther also believed that people are saved by faith and by God's grace. This was opposed to the view that faith and good works were both necessary. Additionally, Luther didn't accept all the sacraments that the Roman Catholic Church did, although the Roman Catholic Church didn't formally fix its number of sacraments (seven) until the aforementioned Council of Trent.

Calvinism is another example of Reformation theological diversity. John Calvin, the founder of Calvinism, believed that all persons are predestined by God to go to heaven or hell. Unsurprisingly, he thought that this was what the Bible taught, and he used scripture to make his case. This was a radically different teaching, as well. Needless to say, the Western Church didn't accept this teaching, either.

You can see that this period in history saw a new proliferation of different interpretations of Christianity. Many more Christian churches that are common today have their roots in the Reformation. Calvin's work was very influential for the Presbyterians. The Church of England (the Anglican Church) also dates from this period, and the Methodists later split off from the Church of England.

In some ways, this period was like a return to the earliest centuries of Christianity, when there was a profusion of different groups that had different understandings of Christianity. Perhaps there is a lesson in here somewhere. The interesting point is that, historically, many of these churches have not reconciled. They continue to go their separate ways. Despite everything, there was a big problem of order within the church, and diversity proliferated again.

That brings us to today. We are used to seeing a large number of different Christian churches. The number has grown, and the theological diversity has increased. New examples include the Christian Scientists and the New Thought movement. The Mormons also belong on this list.

Right now, you might be thinking that the fracturing of Christianity into the tens of thousands of denominations we see today is a horrible thing. All is not lost, however. There have been attempts to reunify some of the churches. This is what *ecumenism* is all about. The word *ecumenism* recalls the ecumenical councils we've looked at, but here the word refers to a different aspect of unity. It's about talks between the churches to see if they can reunite. Eastern Orthodox churches and the Roman Catholic Church have had such a dialog. The Lutherans have talked with the Roman Catholics as well. No grand reunion has taken place yet, but at least there has been a recognition that reunion is in some sense desirable.

To sum up, our brief survey of church history has shown us just how diverse Christianity was in its earliest days and how equally diverse it remains. We've also seen that there have been a lot of thorny issues that Christianity has had to face, and we've seen how Christians tried to deal with these issues. Seeing how Christianity evolved over the centuries is important because it gives you the context for where you are now as a Christian with the particular beliefs you have. Now you have a better idea of where you came from and the history behind your faith.

As I said earlier, what I've shared here is only a modest sample of the diversity of Christian beliefs. If you walked into an imaginary early Christian bookstore, you would find a bewildering array of things to choose from. Here, too, we are lucky, because our early Christian bookstore exists today in digital form on the internet. A vast number of early Christian writings are available to read for free in English translations. To take a look, go to this Web page: http://www.earlychristianwritings.com. I think you'll find looking at this site to be an eye-opening experience. You'll probably be amazed at what you'll find!

# 5

# WORSHIP

Religions don't just give people a set of beliefs and practices to follow. They give us a complete story of everything: who we are, where we came from, why we're here, what to do, and where we're going. That's a lot. The story doesn't end there, though, because all of these things create worlds in which we live. These worlds can be much fuller than we realize.

Think about your own experience. You may go to church several times a week. In between are Bible studies. There are social events with other members of your church. The music you listen to might need to have the Christian stamp of approval: the artists must be Christian, and the lyrics must have a Christian message. You might watch religious programming on TV. You might listen to Christian radio or read Christian books. All of this is aimed at living the Christian life more fully.

You may have also gone to religious schools. These schools have a certain culture and likely feature regular worship services. It's possible to go from elementary school all the way through college in institutions of the same church. Finally, you may remember movies or TV shows that you weren't supposed to see because they were anti-Christian or immoral. All these things go far in keeping you inside the confines of your church, and inside the world your religion creates.

It's easy to see how these factors can affect the kind of person you are. That's the intention, after all. But what if I told you that what Christianity has done goes far beyond all the things I just talked about? What if I told you the way Christians created worlds in the past was far more sweeping? What if I told you that much of what they did still holds true today? You might find that a bit hard to believe. Still, it's quite true, and the center of it all is worship.

It's not easy to determine where to begin the story. Worship itself is a difficult thing to pin down. However, the story of Christian worship must start with the story of Jesus. There would be no Christian worship without Him.

It's important to remember that Jesus was a Jew. That may seem obvious, but what's not so obvious is that Judaism already had its own established worship practices. It had holy days and temple sacrifices. Jesus would have been familiar with these, and he undoubtedly participated in Jewish religious life. The Last Supper, after all, was the celebration of Passover—one of the most important holy days in the Jewish year.

Jesus did something astonishing, however. It happened at the Last Supper.

Many churches celebrate the Last Supper in some form or another. We're all familiar with it. But Passover, which is the origin of the Last Supper, was a Jewish liturgy. It had an established ritual and meaning. What Jesus did was radical: he took that Jewish liturgy and changed it into something new. The change wasn't just to implement an act to remember him (which would be true whether you believe in the real presence in the bread and wine or not). Jesus used the Passover to institute the new covenant.

The old covenant was obviously a major event in Jewish history. It was a solemn agreement between God and his people. The claim that Jesus was making a *new* covenant is shocking. Jesus would have to be God to do such a thing. To use the established Passover liturgy as the occasion just adds more fuel to the fire. How dare Jesus change something so important! Imagine what would happen if someone came into your church and announced that the service was now going to mean something completely different. I doubt that many people would think that was just fine.

But that's exactly what Jesus did. The apostles evidently accepted it. The Lord's Supper thus set in motion much of the history of Christian worship.

In the Jewish tradition, Passover is called the *Pesach*. This is translated into Greek as *Pascha*. Our word *paschal* comes from this translation. The Pesach commemorates God's freeing the people from slavery. Christianity gave new meaning to this, seeing the Pascha as the celebration of Christ's freeing humanity from a different sort of slavery.

The Pascha is the origin of what we presently celebrate as Easter. The Pascha thus came to be one of the first great Christian holy days. It was also the most important one. As Christianity grew, other holy days were added. These, too, were sometimes adapted from Jewish holy days. The idea behind these days was to remember Jesus's life and the salvation that He brought to humanity. All of this was instrumental in the formulation of the *liturgical year*. The liturgical year commemorates that salvation history. That salvation history also changed how Christians understood time. And changing the nature of time was one key to creating a new Christian world.

What makes all this work is the Judeo-Christian understanding of God. For the Jews, God was active in history. He intervened to do things like free his people from slavery in Egypt or part the Red Sea. Israel's God was not distant and aloof. He changed history into salvation history by doing things like these.

The Christian God is the same God, as we know. This God didn't stop doing things in history, either. He sent Jesus to redeem us, incarnating in the process, and after the Resurrection, as the Book of Acts recounts, he sent the Holy Spirit to form the church. This day—Pentecost—became another important day in Christian worship.

Pentecost was another Jewish holy day that was "remade" by Christians. In the Jewish tradition, the feast of Shavuot is celebrated fifty days after Passover. Shavuot is a harvest festival. It celebrates the first gatherings of the harvest. There is a parallel here with the Holy Spirit bringing forth its fruits. Regardless, Christians soon took this day from the Jewish liturgical calendar and made it a major feast day of their own.

Speaking of calendars, an interesting controversy sprang up in the early church with respect to when to celebrate Easter. This disagreement over the date was known as the Quartodeciman (which means the "fourteeners") controversy. Some felt that the Jewish calendar should be followed. This meant that Easter would always fall on the fourteenth day of the Jewish month known as Nisan. That also meant that Easter might fall on a weekday. Others felt that Easter should always fall on a Sunday because Sunday was the day to commemorate the Resurrection. The Council of Nicaea wanted to see all of Christendom celebrate Easter on the same day, but the disagreements prevented the council from completely resolving the matter.

The reason why is rather involved. A big part of it had to do with how time was calculated and measured with calendars. The early church didn't all use the same calendar. Even today, there are at least two different calendars in use in Christendom, and each gives a different date for Easter. Most of us follow the Gregorian calendar (which is named after Pope Gregory XIII, who enacted it). However, much of the Orthodox Church uses the Julian calendar (named for Julius Caesar, who instituted it), which gives a different (usually later) date for Easter.

Just the same, more holy days were added to the Christian liturgical calendar. These often commemorated key events in Jesus's life, including Epiphany, Advent, Christmas, and the transfiguration. Holy days were also added for Mary, Jesus's mother. These filled out the liturgical year even more. Jesus's life history became salvation history.

A regular cycle of holy days thus came together. The liturgical year was further divided into seasons, such as the Christmas season and the Easter season. Easter itself was stretched out to an entire week, climaxing in Holy Thursday, Good Friday, and Easter Sunday. Some churches added a time of fasting before Easter.

Time thus began taking on a different character and a different meaning for Christians. As historical time went on, sacred time was steadily becoming more fully realized. Sundays that were not already great feast days still had a special meaning because every one of them was a remembrance of Easter Sunday, the day of Jesus's resurrection. Sundays were also the first day of the week, which symbolizes the Creation, or the beginning of time. These things made Sundays especially significant.

The liturgical year for some churches also featured feast days for saints, apostles, and martyrs. Additionally, some churches added days to their liturgical calendars to celebrate local saints who were important to them. All these persons were remembered regularly.

Christianity's shaping of time continued to become even more detailed. Many churches devised a standard schedule of Bible readings to be used for worship. These books are called *lectionaries*. This schedule sometimes takes three years to complete. If your church has A, B, or C Bible readings, then it's using a lectionary. Of course, some churches don't follow this practice. It's up to the pastor or whomever leads worship to pick the Bible passage to be used and to preach a sermon on it. For those churches that use lectionaries, though, reading the entire Bible on a regular schedule is just one more way to relive and remember the entirety of salvation history.

So far, we have a liturgical year that is divided into the major holy days and the other feast days, with every Sunday being an Easter in its own way. Revolving around this is a cycle of readings that recounts all of salvation history, going back to its Jewish roots. This gives us a three-year structure of Christian time.

But Christianity didn't stop there in its efforts to shape time. Each day was also divided into times for prayer and worship. If you've ever attended a vespers service (I remember these from Boy Scout summer camp), then you've had a taste of this.

Vespers is only part of a much more extensive structure of daily prayer. The inspiration for this structure is the biblical injunction to "pray without ceasing" (1 Thess 5:17). People took this verse quite seriously and quite literally. As a result, regular periods of daily prayer were devised.

These daily periods of prayer came to be known as *canonical hours*. In some circles, they are known as the Liturgy of the Hours or the Divine Office. Historically, all Christians prayed these hours publicly. These hours were also the basis for prayer in some monastic communities.

Canonical hours took on several forms because different churches devised their own formulas. At the high end of the spectrum, Christians were expected to pray seven or even eight times *every day*. Here is an example of those hours:

matins
lauds
prime
terce
sext
none
vespers
compline

These prayer times were spaced out throughout the entire day and could be supplemented by Mass. A nice article that summarizes the different ways of structuring the hours is here: https://www.britannica.com/topic/divine-office.

Much of this prayer was centered on the Psalms, although sometimes other elements were added. Just as we saw with the readings at services, the readings used for daily prayer were also codified. They were put into books called *breviaries*. The Christian practice once again mirrored the Jewish practice of praying several times a day.

The whole picture of Christianity's understanding of time should now be clear. There is a yearly cycle that remembers the crucial events in the life of Jesus and the life of the church. There is a weekly cycle beginning with the Sunday remembrance of Easter. Then there is the daily cycle of prayer that sanctifies each part of the day. Time has now become Christian time. It has become sacred. Living in time that has been transformed by God's saving action in Jesus is one way in which a new Christian world was created.

But time is only one element of any world. Space is another. For me, teaching James F. White's book *Introduction to Christian Worship* (3rd ed., Abingdon Press, 2000) opened my eyes to just how far Christianity went to use space and time to make its world tangible. If you're structuring time and space, you're structuring lives. If you're structuring lives, you are in a real sense structuring the persons who live those lives. That's the point, too, and it's how Christians tried to set themselves apart and fully live the Christian life. White's book is the inspiration for this chapter.

The Christian use of space was symbolic in many instances. It was another element that Christians manipulated in order to make their world concrete. Of course, there is nothing new about the idea of holy places or sacred spaces. Christians simply did what other religions have done in an effort to make their faith world as real as possible.

The Christian approach to space started simply. You only need to look at the oldest known Christian church to realize this. This is the Dura-Europos church, and it is located in what is now Syria. It dates from the third century. What's interesting about this church is that it is a house church. Early Christians were still being persecuted, so they couldn't build grand church buildings. Because of that, they met in homes. At Dura-Europos, someone took a house and remodeled it to serve as a Christian place of worship. They created spaces in it for different purposes. Wikipedia has a detailed article on this church that includes several photos. It's online here: https://en.wikipedia.org/wiki/Dura-Europos_church.

Much came from these humble house church beginnings. Church architecture and the Christian creation of sacred space became much more elaborate. I want to illustrate this by giving you a few examples. In particular, I want to show you how Gothic cathedrals and Greek Orthodox churches manipulate space to create a Christian world. As you read these examples, I want you to think about how your church shapes space. A lot of theology goes into the creation of Christian space.

Gothic cathedrals have a lot going on, and all of it is quite remarkable. For starters, Gothic cathedrals are all shaped like a cross.

What's more, the top of that cross always points east. East, of course, is the direction of the rising sun. Needless to say, this is symbolic of the risen Son.

What people would probably notice first about a Gothic cathedral is the tall spires that try to reach all the way up to heaven. This isn't a fanciful notion. The reason why it isn't just fanciful is the theology behind these churches. To understand that theology, we'll have to take a short side trip.

There are two theological perspectives we need to consider, and both of them have to do with ecclesiology. The first is *immanence*, and the second is *transcendence*. These roughly correspond to the *earthly* and the *heavenly*. Naturally, the earthly and the heavenly are two different things a Christian can focus on. Gothic cathedrals are built according to the transcendent view. This means the focus is on our future destiny in heaven, not our present situation on earth. Transcendence is also a perspective on God. The transcendent view is of a mysterious God in a distant and mysterious place.

Gothic cathedrals are literally shaped to emphasize this. Not only do you have the tall spires tapering away at the top, but you also have the high, arched ceilings inside. Cavernous ceilings are an effective way to evoke a distant heaven that's "way up there."

The theological elements in the design are fleshed out even more in the stained glass windows. Stained glass windows are something we usually don't think twice about, unless they are especially pretty, perhaps because of the way the sun shines through them. In a medieval cathedral, however, they were far more important. Most of the people in the medieval world were illiterate. The stained glass windows served as teaching aids for these people. You could look at a window depicting an apostle doing what that apostle was known for, and it brought the lesson to life for the average peasant. A carefully laid-out sequence of windows could tell a whole story.

The acoustics of Gothic cathedrals were also designed in a very specific way. They were designed to maximize the effect of the liturgical music of the day. That music was Gregorian chant.

We could spend an entire chapter just talking about sacred music in general and Gregorian chant specifically. This type of music is very different from traditional hymns or gospel music. The point, however, is that the acoustics of Gothic cathedrals were tuned to reinforce the sound of the chant. This created an otherworldly effect. If you've ever heard a recording of Gregorian chant that was made in a Gothic cathedral (or if you've ever heard the same live), you'll understand what I'm talking about. It's quite powerful.

All this was part of the design. Upon setting foot in a Gothic cathedral for mass, you would be in the bottom of the "cross." The priest would be far away, up where the two "beams" intersect. His back would be to the people unless he was delivering the homily (the sermon). His position was that of the intercessor between the people and that distant God. The Mass would be in Latin, which was the "world language" of the Western Church (this was yet another way to create a different, Christian world). The high arched ceilings, the incense, the music, and the stained glass windows would combine with the rest to create a taste of heaven. It would indeed have been mysterious and otherworldly. The world you would be stepping into would have been radically different from the one outside.

Art, music, and architecture thus came together to express a theological vision of the Christian world, making it as concrete as possible. The space inside a Gothic cathedral was transformed into sacred space. Combine that with the transformation of time that we have already discussed, and you get a vivid idea of the new world that Christianity created. You would now be in both sacred time and sacred space.

The Gothic cathedral experience provided the religious multimedia experience of its time for much of Christendom. In our time, *multimedia* means something different. We are probably all familiar with screens in churches that display content that is stored on a computer. We are also probably familiar with electrified musical instruments. The music and the content on the screens might be synced, and there might be lighting effects. Some churches even have stadium seating. Worship services that employ elements like these sometimes resemble concerts. These are our present-day attempts to produce a certain effect. There is undoubtedly a theology driving these choices as well. What kind of Christian world are these modern approaches trying to create?

The second example of sacred space I want to give you is an Orthodox church. This type of structure, which is usually known as a basilica, is quite different from a Gothic cathedral, but no less intricate. It, too, has a strong theological statement to make.

It would take quite a while to describe all the symbolism present in an Orthodox church. The richness and detail here are immense. What I want to do is focus on just some of the elements to give you an idea of what's going on with the building.

To begin with, Orthodox churches are also sometimes cross shaped, although the bottom of the cross may not be as long as what you would see in a Gothic cathedral. The distinguishing feature of many Orthodox churches is their dome or domes. The largest dome, if there is more than one, is likely over the place where the altar is located. This space, called the *sanctuary*, is the most holy part of the church, and you'll also usually find this at its eastern end, just as we saw with the Gothic cathedral. It's where the bread and wine are prayed over to become the body and blood of Jesus.

The dome serves much the same function as the high-arched ceilings in a Gothic cathedral. It evokes heaven. One of the most distinctive features of an Orthodox church will often be on the ceiling of the main dome. What you'll see there is an immense icon of *Christ*

*Pantocrator* that covers the entire ceiling. *Christ Pantocrator* translates to "Christ the ruler of all," or something with the same general meaning. This icon gives you a vivid depiction of Christ in heaven ruling over all of creation. He's also present with the assembled church.

At this point, I need to say something about icons. Icons look like religious pictures to those who don't know about them. They might seem a little strange, too. However, icons are not mere representations of holy persons. They are meant to be means by which you can actually connect with the person depicted in the icon. The people who make icons are required to undergo special theological training so that they can properly make them. Icons are symbols that make available what they portray. As such the icon of Christ Pantocrator becomes an even more powerful symbol.

Next to the sanctuary is the *nave*. This is where the people are gathered for the liturgy. The church assembles here, but the space is less holy than the sanctuary. Only the person leading the worship service and those with permission may enter the sanctuary.

Next to the nave, at the entrance to the church, is the *narthex*. This area is less holy than the nave. In the past, people who were not yet baptized had to stay in the narthex. They were not allowed to enter the nave because they were not yet full members of the church. However, this is not as universally true now as it has been historically.

Between the sanctuary and the nave you'll find an icon screen. The icon screen will always be in front of the sanctuary because it emphasizes the status of the sanctuary as the holiest part of the church. As the name suggests, there are icons on the icon screen, and some of them will be found on all Greek Orthodox icon screens. On the right side will be icons of Jesus and John the Baptist. On the left side will be an icon of Mary the mother of Jesus. In Orthodox Christianity, Mary is venerated as the *Theotokos*. "Theotokos" is Greek for "God bearer." This term emphasizes Mary's role in bearing Christ in her womb. This is crucial because it emphasizes the fact that God became human in order to save us. Other icons typically appear on the icon screen as well, especially if the screen is large.

The icon screen makes the persons depicted on it present. There may be other icons in other parts of the church, as well. What the icons do is connect heaven and earth. The persons depicted on the icons are actually present with the people who are celebrating the liturgy. In this way, the entire church is unified: the people in heaven and the people still on earth. It's a powerful thing.

There is even more detail in an Orthodox church, as I said. Some of it again reflects the Jewish heritage of Christianity. The three-part layout of an Orthodox church, for example, is based on the layout of the Jewish temple. The sanctuary is the holy of holies. But combined with the incense and the sacred Orthodox music, the effect is profound, and mirrors what you would find in a Gothic cathedral in the medieval period. In both, you can see how a theological vision is expressed in the physical world.

The theology expressed by a Greek Orthodox church is therefore more immanent than transcendent. The focus is on the earthly church. Other church buildings can embrace the immanent perspective even more radically, however. What would that look like?

It may look like your church, if your church building is simple and relatively free of decoration or symbolism. The converted storefront church is a good example. The reason why is that the emphasis is on the people, not the building. The theology is that God is present in his people, dwelling within and among them here on earth. If that is the focus of a church's theology, then the elaborate symbolism of the Gothic cathedral or the Greek Orthodox church isn't necessary.

Some churches communicate the immanent point of view by having the altar in the center of the space with the people seated around it. This is the opposite of the Orthodox practice, where the congregation is separated from the holiest space by the icon screen, and it is different from the Gothic cathedral where the altar is in front of the people. The music may be different, as well. After Vatican II, for example, guitar Masses became popular in the Roman Catholic Church.

Some churches will not have pictures of any holy persons in the church building. They consider that to be idolatry. They may have stained glass or other images, but never pictures of Jesus or the apostles or any other religious person. This has been a controversy in Christianity for centuries. The Eastern Church was torn by a major iconoclastic conflict before it decided that icons were acceptable. For a time, though, any icon depicting a religious person was destroyed. As you can see, whether or not to display images such as icons in a church is yet another theological question that determines how space for worship is fashioned.

Our look at the Christian use of space wouldn't be complete without considering a new kind of space for worship: cyberspace. Christians have been very industrious when it comes to the internet. The net has done the same thing that television services once did, offering livestreaming or video recordings of worship services. Online or televised services are handy for people who can't physically attend.

Your church may have an online presence. What's more, it may also take advantage of social media such as YouTube, Facebook, and Instagram. It may host blogs and podcasts. It may even have an online prayer chain. Here's an example of one: https://www.prayerchainonline.net.

Did you know that there are churches whose presence is *entirely* online, though? These churches have no physical buildings at all, but they have tens of thousands of members. You can find a list of some of the biggest ones here: https://blog.capterra.com/the-5-biggest

-online-churches/. There are even online communion services that you can follow. Here's a link to one: https://aboundant.com/interactive-online-liturgy-for-the-sacrament-of-holy-communion/. Is partaking in communion this way legitimate? *Christianity Today* magazine apparently thinks so. You can preview their take on the subject here (you need to subscribe to read the whole article): https://www.christianitytoday.com/ct/2020/march-web-only/online-communion-can-still-be-sacramental.html. Finally, there are resources that people can use to set up online churches. As you might expect, these include apps. This website has an extensive list: https://www.vancopayments.com/egiving/blog/online-worship-resources.

As you can see, the online infrastructure is well developed for Christianity. As an aside, Christianity isn't the only religion that has leveraged the internet. Other religions have also taken advantage of the possibilities that it offers.

It may be too early to tell what cyberspace does to sacred space. It's clear that internet Christianity is here to stay, though. There is no denying the power of the internet. This is no less true for online evangelism. There are sites dedicated to this as well. This one has a good overview: https://www.centerforonlineevangelism.org/what-is-online-evangelism/.

By now I hope you can see that there is a wide variety of approaches to time and space that Christianity has taken, and a wide variety of ways Christianity has taken to creating (or living in, if you prefer) the new creation that Jesus wrought. All of this brings us back to the central notion of interpretation, however. The examples I've shared in this chapter should bring home just how much interpretation shapes your experience of faith, especially when it comes to worship.

As Christians, we recognize (what is usually) the Sunday service as the major service we observe. However, White's book points out that there are other forms of liturgy that are recognized by certain churches, and we need to be aware of these, too. These forms of liturgy add more to the worlds that Christianity creates. Events that are regularly ritualized, like baptism, marriage, and ordination, can also be considered to be liturgical. If a church has a rich array of sacraments that it observes, then it is likely to be a more liturgically oriented denomination. This, too, reflects the church's theology. It's really a matter of how a particular denomination organizes and acts out its understanding of Christianity.

A look at the offices within a church gives us a final clue about worship. How many offices are there? Is there a detailed hierarchy of bishops, priests, presbyters, pastors, lectors, deacons, or ministers? Some of these are mentioned in the Bible. These offices are often involved in worship, and also serve as examples of how worship embodies theology. The offices have clearly defined roles.

The offices in a church don't just pertain to worship and ministry, however. They also reflect the denomination's understanding of authority. Historically, some churches held tightly to a view that their authority came from the apostles, perhaps going all the way back to Jesus himself. Others took a different view, perhaps believing that local or scriptural authority was primary. The ultimate source of authority in a denomination will affect everything that a church does. Planning and leading worship will only be one of the areas this will touch.

All of this brings us back to the central point I made in the first chapter: if you can show me how your church worships, I can show you what your church believes. Worship is an ecclesiological matter. By now you should see the tremendous amount of theology or interpretation that's packed into something as simple as Sunday's service. The time, the space, the people involved, and what they do all say something about that church's understanding of Christianity.

Here are some questions you can ask to explore this for yourself. How many people are involved in leading the service? Just the pastor, or are there others, such as the choir leader, readers, or deacons? Where does their authority to lead worship come from? Are there laypeople involved? Are women allowed to lead worship? Is the person leading the service wearing any vestments? If so, do they display any symbolism? The colors or symbols typically mean something. How are the people in the congregation dressed? "Sunday best" or jeans both make a statement about the relationship between God and the people.

How is your church's space organized? Is there a plan to it? What kind of art is in the space? Is any kind of art forbidden? What kind of music is used? Why is that kind of music used? What is the church's understanding of time? All of these things speak volumes about how your church understands itself and how it understands Christianity. In short, it expresses what your church believes and, more to the point, what *you* believe. It gives you *your* version of Christianity.

What happens when you go to church didn't come about by accident. There is a history behind it all, and that history likely had many decision points along the way. Christianity is a dynamic religion. It's still changing in many ways, even when it comes to worship. Recognizing that, and recognizing what's involved in worship, is a big step to take in order to grow as a Christian. The understanding of Christianity embodied in how you worship is ultimately embodied in *you*.

# 6

# SPIRITUALITY

For a long time I considered spirituality to be an optional fourth item on my list of things that Christians need to know about. I saw no problem with biblical scholarship, church history, or worship. That seemed odd to me, though, because spiritual theology was my area of concentration when I did my master's degree in theology, and spiritual formation was something that I thought was very important. Indeed, one of my pet peeves was that Christian churches were not doing a good job at all of fostering spiritual formation in their members.

Whatever the reason, I finally (recently) came to the conclusion that spirituality and spiritual theology are things that every Christian must know about if they want to grow. Christian spirituality is another immense topic that we can hardly do justice to here, but I think there is a good place to start. That place is what many Christians think being spiritual is all about. I want to start here because there is a great contrast between this and a lot of what's in the tradition of Christian spiritual practice and experience.

So let's begin with a commonsense question: What does it look like to be a really spiritual Christian? It's a simple question, but one that's not easy to answer. One could talk about "putting on the armor of God," as Ephesians 6:11–17 says. The answer might mention having the fruits of the Spirit listed in Galatians 5:22. Another approach is to stand ever more fully on the Word, or be more deeply rooted in it. Of course, the most important thing is to be more like Christ, right?

These aren't necessarily bad ideas. Unfortunately (or fortunately, as the case might be), things are more complicated. I can illustrate this for you by adding a second question to the one I just asked: What might you learn from the massive record of Christian spiritual experience that is recorded in Christian spiritual writing?

You are doubtlessly aware that there are many books you can read that teach you how to be more Christian or help you be a better Christian. But how would you be affected if you read the works of the Christian mystics? What would happen to you if you practiced hesychastic prayer? What would you be like if you went far down the road of *theosis*? I suspect that you and your understanding of Christianity would be very different. Such differences are the kinds of things I want to talk about in this chapter. We're going to go deeper.

Let's begin again in a familiar place. If you belong to a strict church, perhaps a Baptist one, you may have been taught that several things are not allowed. Drinking, dancing, card playing, and premarital sex might be on the list. Doing any of them might send your soul plummeting to hell!

There are variations on this theme, too, where certain activities are encouraged. Fasting and prayer are well-known. Living simply or poorly is also common. You have probably heard the biblical message about getting rid of your possessions and following the Lord. Likewise, you are probably familiar with the Bible passage that says it's easier for a camel to go through the eye of a needle than it is for a rich person to enter heaven (that's another one for biblical scholarship, by the way!).

All of these have something in common. You might have sensed a common thread of denial running through them. That thread takes us to a surprising place, though. It reacquaints us with our old friend Plato.

Don't fret if your eyebrows just went up. Here's a surprise, though: that common thread is bigger than just Christianity. It is a universal one that runs through all the world's great religions. It has quite a history within Christianity, too.

Do you remember our discussion about the soul in chapter 4? I mentioned that there would be more to say in our chapter on spirituality. Well, here we are!

Remember that Plato advised his readers to practice dying so that at death their souls could more easily go where they belonged. Also recall that Plato laid many of the ills of the world at the feet of the body. Perhaps the picture is becoming clearer now. In plain language, what we're talking about is self-discipline or self-control. This should sound familiar. But there is another name for this discipline. It's one that's familiar to scholars of religion and fervent Christians alike. That name is *asceticism*.

The dictionary that comes with my computer (*The New Oxford American Dictionary*, 3rd ed.) defines *asceticism* like this: "severe self-discipline and avoidance of all forms of indulgence, typically for religious reasons." People who practice asceticism (they're called *ascetics*) renounce worldly goods for a higher spiritual good. Worldly goods don't last forever, but the spiritual good (being in heaven with God, for Christian ascetics) does. It's a better thing to strive for.

This gives rise to the old saying about fleeing the world, the flesh, and the devil. Ascetics give up wearing fine clothes, eating gourmet food, and experiencing sexual pleasure. They usually live in poverty and don't want to have a lot of money. They do all this so they can concentrate on becoming more holy, and on trying to get closer to God.

In Christianity, many of the people who seek this kind of life go off to join monasteries or convents. To become full monks or nuns, they will also make formal vows. Typically, vows have three parts: poverty, obedience, and celibacy. Sometimes a vow of stability is added, which basically means the person must stay in the monastery. Obedience, of course, means submission to the authority of the church.

Monks and nuns feature prominently in many of the world's great religions. Buddhism has monks and nuns. Daoism has a monastic tradition. The Essenes of the Dead Sea Scrolls fame were probably a monastic order. Hinduism has a tradition of ascetics and holy persons. Islam has something like this in the various groups that practice Sufism (Sufism is basically Islamic mysticism).

Monasticism is a big part of Christian history. Its rise began when Christians were no longer being persecuted and Christianity became the religion of the Roman Empire. The "red martyrdom" of persecution and death was replaced by the "white martyrdom" of renouncing the world. Many Christians fled to the desert, especially in Egypt, in order to pursue a more fervent spiritual life. Some of them lived alone, and some of them formed communities. All of this really got going in the fourth century.

The people who formed monastic communities were known as *cenobites*. Those who lived alone were known as *eremites*. Our word *hermit* comes from the latter. People living in monasteries or convents can also essentially live the hermitic life there if their journey takes them to a deeply contemplative or mystical place.

The people who formed communities found a need to have a code to live by and a way to regulate their life together. This eventually gave birth to the various monastic rules that became the foundations for these groups, such as the Rule of Benedict (St. Benedict founded the Benedictine Order, and his rule is used by other orders as well). These rules were generally written by the group's founder, and they tried to capture the particular spiritual gift (the theological word for this is *charism*) he or she had. New groups have been formed throughout the church's history, too. Mother Teresa of Calcutta founded the Order of the Missionaries of Charity in 1950, for example.

Different groups (these became known as *orders*, as you might have guessed) focused on different things. Some were more active in the world, like the Jesuits, and some were more contemplative, like the Carthusians. All of them reflected a desire to live the Christian life more deeply and fully. The same thing is true of monks and nuns in other religions. All of these people are trying to live the spiritual life more completely.

Life in a monastery often follows a regular pattern of work and prayer. The prayer part looks much like the Liturgy of the Hours we talked about in chapter 5 on worship. The work the monastics do supports the needs of the monastery. You may be familiar with beer that's brewed in monasteries, for example. Both work and prayer create a life that is focused more fully on spiritual growth. Being apart from the rest of the world helps to foster that growth.

Much Christian spiritual and mystical writing comes from people who lived the ascetic life. Christian mysticism is something that few are familiar with, but it does shine a light on where your journey with God could take you. A word of warning is in order, though. Some of this writing is not what you might expect. It might not even sound very Christian, but it is. If your church doesn't forbid drinking, you might want to take a strong shot before you read any further!

It shouldn't surprise you much now, but once again Plato gets credit for being a huge influence on Christian spirituality. This time, though, it's more for his influence on other people. These people, whom we met before, are the Neoplatonists.

Neoplatonism was a school of philosophy that sought to expand on the work of Plato (and to some extent Aristotle, but that's a philosophy story). There were several Neoplatonic philosophers, but one stands out for his influence on Christians. That philosopher's name is Plotinus.

Plotinus was a mystically oriented person himself. His writing expands on Plato's idea that our soul is not where it wants to be if it is associated with an earthly body. For him, our souls yearn to return to what he calls the One. Unfortunately, our souls descended through various levels to reach this earthly realm, and must traverse various levels to return to the One.

You can see parallels with Christian belief right there. For example, the One clearly resembles God, and this certainly was a connection Christian mystics picked up on, as we'll see.

Plotinus, as well as other Neoplatonic philosophers such as Proclus, strongly shaped the vision and work of arguably the most influential spiritual theologian of the Christian tradition. The name of that man is Dionysius the Areopagite.

We don't know much about Dionysius. His books are named after the Dionysius the Areopagite mentioned in Acts 17:34, but he is almost certainly not that person. Dionysius is generally thought to have lived in the sixth century, which is obviously quite a bit later than the Dionysius mentioned in Acts. Today we might be outraged at the thought of someone writing a book and putting someone else's name on it as the author's name, but the ancient world was much different. Putting the name of a well-known person on your writing was a way to get more attention for it, and the practice was not uncommon. As a matter of fact, the same thing happened with some of the writings in the Bible. Many scholars agree that not all of Paul's letters in the New Testament were actually written by Paul. At any rate, because of this, Dionysius is sometimes referred to as Pseudo-Dionysius (or Pseudo-Denys) just to clarify things.

Not all the books that Dionysius wrote have survived. We have four of his books, plus some letters. There is evidence for seven lost works, as well. Regardless, the books that we do have detonated like a bombshell in the Christian world.

If you were to pick up these books and have a look, you would probably be confused. It might seem like Dionysius is talking about Christianity, but doing so in a strange way. If you looked more closely, you'd find language that seems downright bizarre or even not Christian at all. That's the nature of mystical writing, though. It's a genre all its own. Let me explain.

Mystics are different because they don't rely on intellectual knowledge of the Divine. Instead, they have directly experienced it. In Christian terms, this means they have had an overwhelming experience of the living God. Now, God is God, and we all know that he is incomprehensibly great. So it makes perfect sense to say that the direct experience of God is so overwhelming that it literally can't be put into words. The word for this is *ineffable*. You simply can't put God into the box of language. God's nature is so radically different that it's impossible for us to fully understand.

How do you communicate this? The answer is to use lots of tense and paradoxical language. Words can't adequately explain the experience, but what they can do is act like signposts pointing the way to the experience. It's all we can do, and that's what you see in a lot of mystical writing.

This gives rise to two approaches to talking about God, and you'll find these words in books about spiritual theology. The first is *kataphatic*, and the second is *apophatic*. These simply mean talking about God in terms of what he is and what he is not, respectively.

The latter gets at the idea that God can't be adequately contained or explained in any language, and this is what you find a lot of in mystical writings, as well. It's what the signposts look like.

Here's a passage from Dionysius's book *On Divine Names* that will give you an idea of what apophatic language looks like (all passages from Dionysius in this chapter are from the Parker translation):

> But, let the rule of the Oracles be here also prescribed for us, viz., that we shall establish the truth of the things spoken concerning God, not in the persuasive words of man's wisdom, but in demonstration of the Spirit-moved power of the Theologians, by aid of which we are brought into contact with things unutterable and unknown, in a manner unutterable and unknown, in proportion to the superior union of the reasoning and intuitive faculty and operation within us. By no means then is it permitted to speak, or even to think, anything, concerning the superessential and hidden Deity, beyond those things divinely revealed to us in the sacred Oracles. For Agnosia, (supra-knowledge) of its superessentiality above reason and mind and essence—to, it must we attribute the super-essential science, so far aspiring to the Highest, as the ray of the supremely Divine Oracles imparts itself, whilst we restrain ourselves in our approach to the higher glories by prudence and piety as regards things Divine. For, if we must place any confidence in the All Wise and most trustworthy Theology, things Divine are revealed and contemplated in proportion to the capacity of each of the minds, since the supremely Divine Goodness distributes Divinely its immeasurableness (as that which cannot be contained) with a justice which preserves

> those whose capacity is limited. For, as things intelligible cannot be comprehended and contemplated by things of sense, and things uncompounded and unformed by things compounded and formed; and the intangible and unshaped formlessness of things without body, by those formed according to the shapes of bodies; in accordance with the self-same analogy of the truth, the superessential Illimitability is placed above things essential, and the Unity above mind above the Minds; and the One above conception is inconceivable to all conceptions; and the Good above word is unutterable by word—Unit making one every unit, and superessential essence and mind inconceivable, and Word unutterable, speechlessness and inconception, and namelessness—being after the manner of no existing being, and Cause of being to all, but Itself not being, as beyond every essence, and as It may manifest Itself properly and scientifically concerning Itself.

The apophatic idea that God can't be captured in language is easy to see in this passage. So is the reference to Plotinus's One and Plato's Good (which is at the top of the more complicated version of Plato's worldview). But how can something not be? Doesn't this fly in the face of our common understanding of God? And what is a superessential something that surpasses the essential?

Speaking of God as not existing and somehow being beyond all being is shocking, but it nicely illustrates the paradoxical nature of mystical writing. It takes the idea that our knowledge of the Divine is "unutterable and unknown" and puts it into practice. You literally have to blow up language to get at the experienced reality of God.

Let's expand on this. Dionysius also likes to say that God can't be known in the ways we usually know things. This certainly sounds like it could be a problem. If things like that fail us, then what have we got left? The answer is a direct experience of God that's a whole different kind of religious experience, and one that Dionysius clearly believes is better. This is a radically different way of having a personal relationship with God. It points to the "inconceivable to all conceptions" and "inconception" that he speaks of. This section of *On Divine Names* fleshes out this idea a bit more:

> Concerning this then, as has been said, the super-essential and hidden Deity, it is not permitted to speak or even to think beyond the things divinely revealed to us in the sacred Oracles. For even as Itself has taught (as becomes Its goodness) in the Oracles, the science and contemplation of Itself in Its essential Nature is beyond the reach of all created things, as towering superessentially above all. And you will find many of the Theologians, who have celebrated It, not only as invisible and incomprehensible, but also as inscrutable and un-traceable, since there is no trace of those who have penetrated to Its hidden infinitude. The Good indeed is not entirely uncommunicated to any single created being, but benignly sheds forth its super-essential ray, persistently fixed in Itself, by illuminations analogous to each several being, and elevates to Its permitted contemplation and communion and likeness, those holy minds, who, as far as is lawful and reverent, strive after It, and who are neither impotently boastful toward that which is higher than the harmoniously imparted Divine manifestation, nor, in regard to a lower level, lapse downward through their inclining to the worse, but who elevate themselves determinately and unwaveringly to the ray shining upon them; and, by

> their proportioned love of permitted illuminations, are elevated with a holy reverence, prudently and piously, as on new wings.

Here the experience of God is also said to be "not only as invisible and incomprehensible, but also as inscrutable and un-traceable, since there is no trace of those who have penetrated to Its hidden infinitude." The person who seeks God is also illumined by a "super-essential ray" according to his or her capacity to receive it. What this boils down to is a way of knowing God that is *much* different from the way you might be used to.

The idea that there is some kind of essence that is better than essences also shows up again in this passage. It's an important point for Dionysius, and it's central to his understanding of God, so it's good for us to take a closer look.

We learned earlier that everything has an essence. An essence is what a thing ultimately *is*. An essence is that without which a thing would not be what it is. The idea that there is something *above* essence sounds like a flat-out impossibility. That, however, is what God "is," and somehow we know this in the mystical experience of him.

What Dionysius is doing is trying to clarify the nature of the Divine. The Divine is clearly a very different kind of thing. Again, its nature is not something we can put into words. The trick (and this is true for all mystics, regardless of what religion they're from) is that you have to experience it to understand it. When you do, it all makes sense.

The passages we've looked at here aren't the only examples of the kind of language mystics use to try to convey their experience of the unfathomable. In *Mystic Theology*, Dionysius writes about Divine darkness, including "the superessential ray of Divine darkness." This should get your attention. We're used to thinking of God as light.

Darkness is evil. Why is Dionysius saying that God is darkness? Is he saying God is evil? That sounds frightening!

It isn't. What he's doing is using different tense and paradoxical language to point out that God is completely beyond our understanding. It's as if the more we experience God as he is, the more mysterious he becomes. We're literally in the dark when it comes to knowing God fully. Dionysius also makes this clear by referring to God as hidden, as we've seen. This kind of talk shouldn't upset us now that we understand what Dionysius is trying to communicate.

Another famous Christian mystical text written in the fourteenth century, titled *The Cloud of Unknowing*, reinforces the notion that God is unknowable. The book uses the title's metaphor to describe the mystical journey into God, which is like going into a cloud. If you've ever flown into a cloud before, you know the feeling of being lost and disoriented. It's a lot like being in thick fog. Here, it's an artful way of communicating the central fact that God is mystery. Being in God is like being lost in a cloud. That's no less true even for people who have had exalted experiences of God. It's one thing to have a doctrine or a theology, but the danger in that is that we might lose sight of just what God really is. The reality of God is so different that we can't even picture for ourselves what it's like, no matter how hard we try. Thankfully, the mystics are there to remind us of that.

Dionysius (and by extension, Neoplatonism) exercised a tremendous influence on Christianity going forward. The Orthodox and Roman Catholics have a feast day dedicated to Dionysius. Thomas Aquinas (we met him earlier) drew heavily on him for the section on God in his masterwork, the *Summa Theologica*. Interestingly enough, later in his life Thomas had a spiritual experience of his own that led him to compare his work to straw. The influential

Christian thinker St. Augustine of Hippo was also heavily influenced by Neoplatonism.

In the medieval period, John Scotus Erigena translated Dionysius's works into Latin. This translation brought Dionysius's work to medieval theologians. Hugh of St. Victor, for example, wrote a commentary on Dionysius's book *Celestial Hierarchy*. Erigena himself wrote intriguing comments on Dionysius's work. These are just a few cases.

These examples of Christian mysticism show what's possible and what's there in Christian spirituality. You might have thought that mysticism was something scary or undesirable, or something that had to do with other religions. That's not entirely true. Now that you know that mysticism is a large part of Christian spirituality, you might be curious about how to get it. What does one do to reach high levels of spiritual attainment? Christianity has answers for this, too. It's where hesychastic prayer comes in.

I want to discuss hesychasm because it is an excellent illustration of advanced Christian spirituality. I'll begin by talking about hesychasm's great historical advocate and teacher, Gregory Palamas. Gregory Palamas was an Orthodox monk and archbishop who lived in the thirteenth and fourteenth centuries. He is recognized as a saint in several Orthodox communions. He is famous not only for his exposition of hesychastic prayer but also for his defense of it during times of great controversy. His efforts were so successful that hesychasm was eventually accepted as orthodox teaching in Orthodox Christianity.

It is difficult to discuss hesychasm without discussing the Jesus Prayer. This prayer is central to the practice. The most well-known form of the prayer that I have found is this: "Jesus Christ, Son of God, have mercy on me, a sinner." A key part of the spiritual practice of hesychasm is to repeat this prayer *constantly*.

The Jesus Prayer can be combined with breathing techniques as well. Either way, the intent is to keep one's attention always on God. Eventually, this produces an interior state that better enables the practitioner to experience God. Hesychasm, in fact, translates as "quiet." That inner quiet opens you up to a better experience of God.

But let's return to Palamas. A central point he makes is that we can never experience the essence of God. For Palamas, that's simply impossible. This looks like a nod to Dionysius. We do experience God's energies, however, so we can directly experience God *somehow*. The distinction between God's essence and his energies is a crucial part of his mystical theology. God's energies are quite powerful, too. They manifest as light, and Palamas thinks this light is the same light the disciples saw when Jesus was transfigured on Mount Tabor.

This light is *uncreated*, though. It's evidence of spiritual transformation. This is where the notion of *theosis* comes in. The goal of hesychasm is to somehow be "divinized" by this encounter with God. Christian theology generally will not allow anyone to say that we can become one with God. That's because it would imply that God lacks something or is incomplete. If that were the case, God wouldn't be perfect. This line of thought, interestingly enough, also has roots in Greek philosophy. In this case, it doesn't come from Plato but from an earlier philosopher named Parmenides.

So the hesychast (this is what practitioners of hesychasm are called) doesn't fully become *one* with God, but his (or her) nature is somehow changed into something better. The hesychast also moves to a place where God's love is experienced. Given that the practice centers so much on an awareness of one's sinfulness, this represents a big change.

Palamas thinks that this kind of spiritual life is not for everyone. It's very demanding, and it's easy to see why. You must be very committed and very focused to attain such high levels of spiritual development. It's there in Christian tradition, however.

This brings us to more "how" with respect to Christian spiritual growth. Actually, it's more of a helpful "what." Spiritual growth passes through several stages. Interestingly enough, there is more than one approach to the stages of the spiritual journey. Let's take a look at two of them.

If you are in a Bible-centered church, you may have heard preaching or teaching around the first approach. The stages here are analogous to the stages of growth all of us go through as human beings. A good example of this teaching can be found here: https://holyjoys.org/three-stages-growth/.

The second approach, which is prominent in Roman Catholic spiritual theology, is different. It's less common, so you might not be familiar with it. In this one, the stages focus more on the inner changes you undergo as you make progress in the spiritual life.

There are three stages in this approach. The three stages are purgation, illumination, and union. These are more evocative of what the spiritual journey does to you. The stages are descriptive, so it should be easy to get a handle on what happens in each.

In the first stage, one begins getting rid of all that is not Godly. Anything that might hold you up on the spiritual path is going to be purged. This process might not be pleasant.

As one continues to move forward, the purging eases and is replaced with experiential knowledge of God. We are "illumined" with this. This isn't an end in itself, even though it might be profound. This stage reflects a growing holiness, or a coming closer to God.

The last stage might be misnamed. As we've discussed, union with God is a theological impossibility. Just the same, your religious experience here will be qualitatively better than the previous stages.

You might experience raptures (not to be confused with the Rapture) or ecstasies or things of that sort. Presumably, this is the sort of thing we are made for.

As you can see, there is quite a lot going on in Christian spirituality. I can't emphasize enough that it's about *religious experience*. It's about much more than just trying to conform yourself to a set of behaviors, commandments, or expectations. It's about the lived experience of the triune God. If you come from a tradition where the Holy Spirit is actually experienced in worship, like Pentecostal or charismatic Christianity, then you have some idea of what this is like. Imagine such an experience that is much more intense, and you'll be going in the right direction.

What stage of spiritual growth are you in? Were you even aware that there were stages of spiritual development? There is a lot more room for spiritual growth in Christianity than you might have realized. This chapter has barely touched on it. All it has done is give you the idea that there is much more, and provided a few examples to illustrate that. The spiritual tradition is something every Christian should know, however. It's your birthright. Now that you have this knowledge, you can begin to explore these resources for yourself. I'll give you some pointers when we wrap things up in the next chapter.

# 7

# CHRISTIAN MATURITY

We've come to the end of our look at the four things every Christian should know in order to become a mature Christian. At this point, I hope you see that there is a lot more to Christianity and to being a Christian than you might have realized. I don't want to end things quite yet, however. I want to put the four components together and then discuss some of the further consequences of what we've learned.

Let's begin with the Bible. To sink more fully into the Bible, you're going to need more than a simple concordance, or maybe even a study Bible. You don't need to be a scripture scholar to be able to mine the Bible's riches, though. There are Bible dictionaries that are good for giving you the background on words and how they've been translated. That's useful. For an explanation of why, check out this page, hosted by Logos: https://www.logos.com/grow/online-bible-dictionaries/. Similarly, there is an abundance of published Bible commentaries that pull together biblical scholarship and can really tell you what's going on with the Bible. I'll say more about these in a moment. I recommend that you take advantage of both if you haven't already.

The situation is much the same when it comes to church history. The websites I have mentioned in chapter 4 are excellent places to read historical material. There are also encyclopedias that cover various topics. Much of this material is historical. Some encyclopedias are also available online for free. Much of what you'll find online may be quite old, though, so it may have limited usefulness.

Worship is a bit trickier. There may not be as much free background material you can access online, but you can compensate with something else: videos of actual worship services. These can expose you to some of the variety in Christian worship.

When I teach my in-person classes, I often have my students attend a church service of a Christian denomination other than their own. I then have them write a paper about their experience, paying special attention to a couple of factors that we've covered in class. You can do the same thing virtually. With the internet, you have an unparalleled opportunity to explore different expressions of Christianity.

Don't forget to explore other Christian material on YouTube, either. There is a lot of video there on all sorts of Christian topics (and material about other religions as well). This is especially true for music. I'm not going to spill the secret here, but you may be very surprised at what you find when you really explore Christian music. With respect to all of it, though, your reach is only limited by how good your internet search skills are.

Finally, spirituality is something that is much easier to learn about in our day and age. One resource that I highly recommend is Paulist Press's *Classics of Western Spirituality* series (https://www.paulistpress.com/Products/CategoryCenter/COWS/all-titles.aspx). What began as a limited set of titles has now expanded into a massive catalog of books covering many different spiritual traditions. These are available in affordable paperback editions. Each book has an up-to-date translation of writings by the figure or topic in question, along with an introduction that gives you background on that person or topic. This series does a major service to those who wish to explore spirituality more deeply.

Many of these resources, and more, are available at libraries. If you happen to live near a good university library, you have access to even more material. You'll generally find the dictionaries and commentaries in the library's reference section. You won't be able to check them out, but you'll still be able to take advantage of the wealth of knowledge they contain.

You need to be careful about choosing these sources, though. This is especially important when it comes to picking Bible commentaries, because these come in several different flavors. Some of them cover just one book of the Bible. Some of them cover the entire Old Testament or the entire New Testament. Some of them cover the entire Bible. More importantly, even commentaries are not immune to the influence of interpretation. This Web page, hosted by the University of Northwestern–St. Paul, tells the tale all too clearly: https://guide.unwsp.edu/c.php?g=57415&p=368139. Commentaries often have a theological or church-specific agenda.

Still, you'll want an up-to-date commentary. There are some that were written centuries ago that people still like, and as I mentioned before, some of these you can access online for free. Scholarship has moved on since then, however, and it's generally a good idea to get the latest findings.

Pay close attention to the author(s) and publishers of the commentaries you're interested in. If the commentary is from a good academic publisher, it's been vetted by an editorial board and is more likely to be a good-quality source. If it's not, it may be harder to determine how good it is.

Choosing a commentary is harder now than it used to be because there are so many available. This Web page, also from the University of Northwestern–St. Paul, should help guide you to the right one: https://guide.unwsp.edu/c.php?g=57415&p=7427502. The pages linked on the navigation menu on the left side of the screen are also very useful.

As a footnote to this discussion, if you've looked at the Bible dictionaries page I linked above, you may have noticed that there are also theological dictionaries. These are useful for those doing in-depth study of theology. If you really get into any of the areas of theology that I talked about earlier, these dictionaries can be quite useful.

One thing I hope you'll ponder as you consider all these resources is just how much there is to learn. Even basic things like deciding the date for Easter have an entire history behind them. Earlier Christians put a lot of thought and work into their decisions, yet they didn't always agree. Keep in mind that the things they dealt with weren't trivial for them, either. To stick with our example, they took determining the date for Easter very seriously.

This was true for pretty much all the early church's major decisions. The early church often engaged in much-heated debate before a matter was settled, and sometimes it got nasty. Things were not nearly as simple as you might have thought! All of this makes for fascinating reading. It's more than that, though—it's your family history as a Christian. It's who you are. You stand on the shoulders of all those who came before you. They did much of the heavy lifting so you don't have to. At the very least, you have an opportunity to learn from them so you don't have to reinvent the wheel.

All of this is a roundabout way of coming back to a central

theme of this book: Christianity is very much about theology. Interpretation gives birth to theology.

This dynamic is true for every religion. One of the first things that happens when a new religion comes on the scene is that it splits into competing schools of thought. These groups can differ quite a bit from one another. This happened to Christianity, as we've seen. We've looked at only a few of the early Christian groups in this book, but there were many others. The creation of new groups hasn't stopped, either.

A brief comparison might bring home the point that division is a regular thing in the world's major religions. Consider Judaism, for example. Judaism, the parent religion of Christianity, has undergone several changes since the time when Jesus walked the earth. This is largely because the temple that was the center of Jewish worship in Jesus's time was destroyed shortly after his death and resurrection. The reason why is that the Zealots (Judas Iscariot was a Zealot, remember) rose up in rebellion against Rome. They lost that war, and the Romans destroyed the temple after laying siege to Jerusalem.

Judaism had to drastically remake itself (again) in order to survive. The result was that you now have three major branches of Judaism. These are the Orthodox, Conservative, and Reform branches. They run the gamut from ultraconservative to liberal.

Islam, the other great monotheistic/Abrahamic religion (something it has in common with Judaism and Christianity) split into three major groups as well. You have probably heard of the Sunni and Shia groups, but you may not be aware of the third. That would be the Sufis. Sufism, as we saw, generally represents the mystical side of Islam. Naturally, there are further divisions within these three as well.

Buddhism also split into competing schools after the Buddha died. There are many Buddhist groups now. Zen (which actually began in China when Buddhism encountered Daoism) and Tibetan

Buddhism are perhaps the most well-known. However, Theravada and Mahayana Buddhism are large and important groups.

Hinduism is harder to categorize because it is so diverse. These days, scholars are even questioning whether the term "Hinduism" really works to describe the religiosity of India. Be that as it may, there are many traditions within it. Some of them center on devotion to a particular god or goddess. There's also the Vedic tradition, which is perhaps the oldest of India's religious traditions. Many of India's scriptures come from it. Advaita Vedanta, on the other hand, is different from the Vedic tradition. Again, these are just a few examples.

Daoism (this is the spelling of Taoism that's more commonly accepted today) also has three major divisions. The first is the Daoist "church." This is an institutionalized form of the religion. The second is often referred to as "philosophical Daoism." That's because Eastern religions sometimes blur the line between religion and philosophy (this is also true for Buddhism, for example). The third major branch of Daoism is alchemical Daoism. Alchemy is an entire subject of its own. Trust me: if you don't know what alchemy is, you probably don't want to know! It can be rather disturbing. Alchemy (which is found in both the East and the West) essentially embodies difficult and potentially dangerous esoteric practices that can result in extreme self-transformation. The Daoists, for example, claim that you can actually become immortal if you follow the road properly to the end. The same idea is found in Western alchemy.

You can see that religious diversity is a fact that a spiritually mature person must contend with. Such a person has to have some kind of understanding of it, and some kind of answer to the question of why it's there. This is true both for the differences in your own religion and for the differences between your religion and all the others. The easy way out is to say that anything that's different from your particular belief is wrong. That raises soteriological questions, though. It also leads to this question: Why do other religions seem to work? After all, they produce people who seem to be righteous and holy. What are we to make of that?

The point I want to make is that nothing is simple. That's another goal of this book. These pages are meant to bring home not only the depth but also the complexity of Christianity. Being mature in your faith means not turning your back on this complexity. You need to embrace it. This might sound like a lot of work or hassle, but there is no getting around the fact that even just Christianity is a massive thing that has a lot going on in it. This has been true for close to two thousand years. The theological and cultural accumulation of centuries of experience of people over most of the earth isn't a minor thing. If you want to grow in your faith, you can't ignore that.

Ecumenism, which we discussed earlier, tries to deal constructively with the Christian part of this complexity. The hard part is that you are dealing with absolute truths. If you're talking about the nature of Jesus Christ, there is no room for error. If you're talking about the fact that Jesus was God incarnate, you can't fudge. That's what Christian history shows us. For many, those truths are written in stone. The church wrestled with hard, complex issues like these precisely because people had different fundamental truths about them. That's why the tradition is so important for what Christianity looks like today. If the beliefs of any of the heretical groups had become the norm, Christianity would look very different, and so would you. Your beliefs would not be the same as they are right now.

A related issue around being mature in your faith is realizing that, many times, the people teaching it may not want to go into such complexity. There are two factors at work here. The first is pretty straightforward. Think of a church full of people on a typical Sunday. Some of them have not had deep teaching in the faith. Some of them may be "cultural Christians" who go to church on Sunday but do little, if anything, to grow in their faith the rest of the week. The pastor doesn't want to drive these people away. Instead, the message that he or she preaches may be formulated to try to reach as many people as possible. So the strategy might be to preach something on the general side hoping to coax people into living a better life.

That brings us to the second factor. People today might not have the patience or desire to seek the kind of deeper teaching they need to grow, especially if that involves spiritual formation. Either that, or what's being taught doesn't cover some of the topics we've covered. Some churches may center their teaching primarily on the Bible and may not deal with things we've looked at here. That's their priority. Either way, you're looking at a large amount of material that people might need to learn. Having a qualified teacher might also be a factor.

That makes sense. Religion is a complicated thing because it deals with every aspect of life. As we all know, life itself is a complicated thing. It's often hard to deal with. Put the two together and you have a lot to handle.

Religion tries to give people answers to that complexity. However, that means the answers themselves can be very complicated. Our look at the areas of theology and at the history of the church gave us hints about just how complicated that can be. But here's the rub: most people don't want to be theologians. Most people aren't the sorts who love to dive into the problems life throws at us to try to devise subtle and nuanced solutions. In short, a lot of people *want* to keep religion simple. It's their rock and their anchor. They may be scared to look more deeply into the thorny problems we all encounter. They may not be inclined to do the work needed to try to come up with better solutions. They may not have the tools to do so, either.

It's easy to show how this works by looking at law and ethics. Law tries to cover all aspects of human behavior in order to dispense justice, but that is extraordinarily difficult to do. Legal codes typically fill several volumes, and vary considerably depending on locale. Secular ethics works in much the same way. It generally tries to establish a code of right and wrong. That's also incredibly hard to do. There are very different ways of doing ethics, and they can arrive at opposite conclusions to one another, with each claiming strong justification for its answers.

Religious ethics has the same problem. It's not easy to conclusively nail down every single aspect of human life in order to have a definitive moral code. Christianity condemns murder, for example, yet some denominations justify it under the just war doctrine. Killing in a war—if the war meets certain specific conditions—is then morally justified. Of course, not all Christians accept this. Christian pacifism is also an established part of Christian history and tradition that goes all the way back to the early days of the church.

However, becoming mature in your faith means facing such issues head on. You need to be willing to delve into the messiness of life and the complexity of the Christian response. It will be more difficult, but it will be worth it because you will have greater understanding and more to draw on to make you stronger. This offers the promise of living a better life.

Who wouldn't want that? It's something we all strive for. What the process of getting there gives us is *wisdom*. Wisdom is an invaluable thing. It's hard to put your finger on just what it is, but it can make a huge difference because you'll be able to deal with life's problems more easily. It can enhance your ability to enjoy life's goodness, too. Christian wisdom is having the ability to do this in an authentically Christian way. It's good for you, and it's something you can pass on to others. That's what being an elder or a church leader should really be about.

In a word, then, I'd say that Christian maturity requires an *informed faith*. That's what the four items I've discussed in these pages will to provide you. Getting to know the scriptures in a fuller way, knowing the history of how Christianity grappled with serious questions, knowing how Christianity creates a world to live in, and knowing what is possible in the spiritual life are all important things. Without them, your potential to grow will be limited. You'll be cut off from things that could open up new horizons for you, and you'll deprive yourself of resources that could make a huge difference in the quality of your spiritual life. It's like climbing the mountain instead of staying in the valley. If you climb the mountain, you'll have a much better view. You can see a lot more from the mountaintop than you can see from the valley.

You won't be able to be informed if you don't ask questions. One of the problems we talked about in our opening chapter was not questioning your religion. That's because people hold on really tight to the "gospel truth" they've been taught, and any perceived movement away from it is seen as dangerous. You might go to hell! People sometimes believe the truth they've been given really is absolute and can't be challenged. But the reality is that people challenge religious truth all the time. Theologians constantly ask questions, for example. As we saw earlier, they may have limits they have to stay within, but they still probe and explore. Believe it or not, plenty of ordinary people ask questions, too. There is a lot of religious flux in the world. People either change religions or just accept the parts of a religion they like. Sometimes they even mix and match elements of different traditions to suit their fancy. This drives religious leaders up the wall, but it's a very real thing. It's another example of the messiness you might run into.

The development of Christianity has been driven by questioning. Our look at early Christian history confirms this. There were many different interpretations of Jesus, and eventually those were called into question by the need to keep the Roman Empire united. Our Christian forebears sorted out these questions, and established doctrine for the whole church. Some of the answers that were floating around were deemed to be heretical, but the important point is that the process of question and answer allowed the church to build a firm foundation of belief.

The same thing happened during the Reformation. People like Martin Luther questioned what was going on in the church because they thought there was a problem. The church didn't treat the reformers well, but in the process it did clean up its act and answer more questions definitively. The reformers wound up starting new churches, and there are many people who obviously accept the reformers's ideas as valid expressions of Christianity. That probably worked for the people in those churches. I don't know if any of you will ever need to take a courageous stand like Luther did and risk excommunication, but his example shows that we can have the courage to question the things we've learned.

It's easy to take our beliefs for granted, but it's good to realize that it was not always so. We now have the benefit of two thousand years of Christian questioning. It would be foolish to ignore that. That's why looking at the history of Christianity as a whole, and not just the history of your own denomination, is an extremely valuable thing to do. It gives you perspective. When you consider how your denomination came to have its beliefs in the light of how and why different denominations came to have theirs, it can be an enlightening experience. It makes you realize how hard it is to pin down truth—even in your own denomination or religion. Knowing about the difficulty involved in trying to do so can help make you more understanding and tolerant. If you are a Christian who wants to see the divided body of Christ reunified, knowing about this problem is a big help. You probably won't get a deeper understanding without a questioning attitude, however.

If you go down the ecumenical highway, you will surely run into that problem of the "gospel truth." It's a real sticking point for those who would like to see the churches reunited. After all, we're dealing with God's revelation to humanity. It's important that we hear it correctly! It's also supposed to be clear, isn't it, so that we all might be saved?

You might have thought so before, but maybe you don't think that so much now! Let's focus more clearly on what you'll run into, though. As I mentioned before, there are tens of thousands of different Christian denominations. I'm confident that every one of them believes it has The Christian Truth, and that even if they admit there are some problems, their approach is likely the best one to find the answer. That means there are *tens of thousands of absolute Christian truths* out there in the world right now. What happened to our clear and simple revelation?

I'm afraid it's that word again that's to blame. You know the word I'm talking about: interpretation. That's the immediate problem. The bigger problem is the understanding of authority that each denomination has. This authority is the basis for each of them saying its belief is absolute. Authority in Christianity is another subject all its own, and it, too, is a major part of Christian history. That's also an issue you might want to research. But it points to the problem all religions have when they try to nail down what the absolute truth is. Do you remember what I said about religions splitting into different factions? Another way of looking at what happened is to realize that there were disagreements over things that some people thought were or should be absolute truths, and other people didn't.

Now I'm not here to solve the problem of absolute truth for you, as tempting as it might be to try. But I do want to suggest that there is a lot of room for disagreement. You may think that your absolute truth really is *the* absolute truth, and that's fine. I'm not going to say that's necessarily wrong. But now that you have more awareness around the issue, you have some context for your decision. Remember, many Christian churches were founded by "heretics," but those churches are still alive and kicking. If you're going to judge that all the people in them are wrong and are going to go to hell, I want you to at least have a better argument for why. The same thing applies to people in other religions, too.

There's one more way of looking at what all this diversity has given us, though. Instead of seeing problems everywhere, you could see it as a wild expression of creativity. That's already there in the religion. Let's be daring and ask a question: *Are all the differences in religion a good thing?* Maybe there's some wiggle room when it comes to absolute truth. Maybe there isn't. But the creativity in understandings of Christianity (let alone other religions) isn't going away anytime soon. It's a fact we need to deal with. If your soteriology is broader, then you can be happy that a Christian with a different understanding from yours will still go to heaven. That might free you up to explore the riches that the other person's denomination has to offer. Multiply this many times over and you begin to see how much you might stand to gain.

I'll illustrate this with an example. Earlier in this chapter, I mentioned the church visit assignment I have in some of my courses. The results of this assignment are often eye-opening. My students are amazed at what they learn. Sometimes they report being exposed to something so completely different that they had a hard time trying to make sense of it. Sometimes they find a church that they like better than the one they have been attending. The results of the assignment have been overwhelmingly positive. My students very often come away with a new and broader understanding. Attending a different church in person, and not just virtually, is something you might want to try for yourself. You'll likely get a fuller experience if you go in person, and that will really drive my point home.

By now, I hope you've realized that a lot of what this chapter (and this book) is about is theological maturity. Theology is unavoidable, as we saw in our second chapter. Theology is what all four of the things on my list are about. Seeing where theology goes, even when it comes to absolute truth, is sobering, but like it or not, that's the way it is.

Theology goes hand in hand with complexity. Theology is unavoidable because complexity is unavoidable. You may wish this wasn't true for Christianity. You may have been taught that Christianity is simple, and you may want it to be that way. But the plain fact is that Christianity isn't simple. Hopefully these pages have made that clear.

The last thing I want to do before we go is to say a few more words about spiritual theology. I'm going to change keys this time because spirituality is very much an internal kind of thing. It's very personal. Given that, there is one guiding principle that I can give you: you can grow a lot in and from the religious experience you have. Your spiritual experience will inform the other three areas on my list. You may begin to see all four of them dance together in beautiful ways.

There are few suggestions I can make when it comes to religious experience and the spiritual life, and this time they're experiential instead of intellectual. The first has to do with prayer. There are actually several kinds of prayer. Many of them will be familiar to you, but it helps to break them down. There are a few kinds that I want to mention here. The first is probably the most common. This is petitionary prayer. Petitionary prayer is just what it sounds like: it's asking God to do something. I suspect this is the type of prayer most people do. The second kind of prayer is similar. This is intercessory prayer. Here you are asking God to intervene on behalf of someone or something. You want Him to act to change something. You can see how this can overlap with petitionary prayer.

The next two kinds of prayer are nonverbal. The first is praying with the Bible. Traditionally, this is called *lectio divina*, which is Latin for "divine reading." It is a way of really using the Bible to grow deeper in the spiritual life. It can fuel spiritual growth. You may already be doing something like this. The second kind of nonverbal prayer is contemplative prayer, which is the act of being caught up in the experience of God. It's the kind of thing mystics experience.

It's important to realize that prayer doesn't have to be an active thing. Just being quiet and alone with God can be a very prayerful experience. Anything can be prayerful if you're focusing on God while you do it.

A final suggestion with regard to spirituality has to do with discernment. Another term for discernment is "testing the spirits." You may be more familiar with that phrase. Regardless of which term you're comfortable with, the idea is important because it has to do with what's going on inside you. It's checking to see that you are still going down the path God wants you to go down. The difference is that the person doing the discerning or testing should have the ability to tell if the experience you are having is from God or not. This may not be easy, and it usually requires someone to be quite experienced in the spiritual life.

In many traditions, these people are called spiritual directors. Sometimes they are known as spiritual friends. These are people who know what you're going through because they've already been there themselves. A spiritually mature person like a spiritual director can really help you stay on track as your spiritual life unfolds. Being such a person yourself is another sign of Christian maturity. Bear in mind the difference between this and an elder or a teacher, however. The religious experience makes the difference. We're not talking about people who have only good intellectual knowledge. They need more than that.

Paying attention to your inner life may well be the hardest part of becoming spiritually mature. I strongly believe that it's the heart of religion, though. That's why I want to end on that note. It really is that important.

At the end of the day, if I were to sum up what this book has been about, I'd put it this way: it's about expanding your religious horizons much farther than you knew they could go. In its own way, this entire book is only a signpost. My goal here is to simply point to the path and give you an idea of what it looks like. I have also offered a few pointers to get you started. In the end, it's up to the Holy Spirit to guide you in the particular way that's best for you. I sincerely hope that happens, and that your mustard seed grows into a mighty tree (Matt 13:31–32). I wish you a fruitful journey!